PUPIL
TEXTBOOK
5B

Ooogol

Noogol

Googol

Koogol

Toogol

Zoogol

Consultant and author
Dr Fong Ho Kheong

Authors
Gan Kee Soon and Chelvi Ramakrishnan

UK consultants
Carole Skinner, Simon d'Angelo and Elizabeth Gibbs

© 2015 Marshall Cavendish Education Pte Ltd

Published by Marshall Cavendish Education
Times Centre, 1 New Industrial Road, Singapore 536196
Customer Service Hotline: (65) 6213 9444
Email: tmesales@mceducation.com
Website: www.mceducation.com

Distributed by
Oxford University Press
Great Clarendon Street, Oxford,
OX2 6DP, United Kingdom
www.oxfordprimary.co.uk
www.oxfordowl.co.uk

First published 2015

ISBN 978-981-01-8897-9

Printed in China

Acknowledgements
Written by Dr Fong Ho Kheong, Gan Kee Soon and Chelvi Ramakrishnan

UK consultants: Carole Skinner, Simon d'Angelo and Elizabeth Gibbs

Cover artwork by Daron Parton

The authors and publisher would like to thank all schools and individuals
who helped to trial and review Inspire Maths resources.

Introduction

Inspire Maths is a comprehensive, activity-based programme designed to provide pupils with a firm foundation in maths and to develop the creative and critical thinking skills to become fluent problem solvers.

Inspire Maths makes learning maths fun and rewarding through the use of engaging illustrations and games that help to reinforce and consolidate learning.

For the teacher:

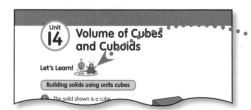

Use the engaging and highly scaffolded **Let's Learn!** to introduce concepts. Integrated questions allow for immediate assessment and consolidation of concepts learnt.

Carry out investigative activities in **Let's Explore!** These allow pupils to apply concepts learnt.

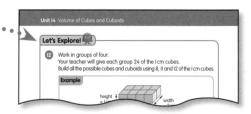

Challenge pupils to solve non-routine questions by applying relevant heuristics and thinking skills in **Put On Your Thinking Caps!**

Indicates that appropriate use of calculators is encouraged for the activities and practices to extend problem-solving skills.

For the parent/guardian:

Build home-school links and make maths come alive by using the tips in Home Maths to help children apply mathematical concepts to daily life.

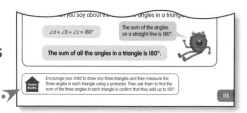

For the pupil:

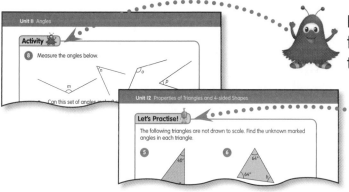

Enjoy **Inspire Maths** with your friends. Explore your learning through activities and group work.

Let's Practise! contains questions that provide opportunities for further practice.

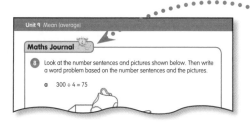

Share what you have learnt, create your own questions and become aware of your own mathematical thinking in your **Maths Journal** .

Recall skills from earlier years and link them to new concepts in the current unit.

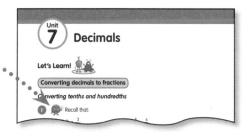

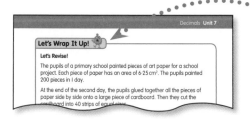

Let's Wrap It Up! summarises the concepts you have learnt in the current unit, while **Let's Revise!** provides a worked example that covers the key concepts for ease of revision.

Contents

Unit 7 Decimals

Let's Learn!

Converting decimals to fractions

Converting tenths and hundredths

1   Recall that:

a $0 \cdot 3 = \frac{3}{10}$ $0 \cdot 8 = \frac{8}{10} = \frac{4}{5}$

$1 \cdot 3 = 1\frac{3}{10}$ $2 \cdot 8 = 2\frac{8}{10} = 2\frac{4}{5}$

$11 \cdot 3 = 11\frac{3}{10}$ $22 \cdot 8 = 22\frac{8}{10} = 22\frac{4}{5}$

b $0 \cdot 07 = \frac{7}{100}$ $0 \cdot 24 = \frac{24}{100} = \frac{6}{25}$

$1 \cdot 07 = 1\frac{7}{100}$ $5 \cdot 24 = 5\frac{24}{100} = 5\frac{6}{25}$

> $\frac{8}{10}$ and $\frac{24}{100}$ can be written in their simplest forms.
>
> $$\frac{8}{10} = \frac{8 \div 2}{10 \div 2} = \frac{4}{5}$$
>
> $$\frac{24}{100} = \frac{24 \div 4}{100 \div 4} = \frac{6}{25}$$

Converting thousandths

2 Recall that:

$0.001 = \dfrac{1}{1000}$

$1.001 = 1\dfrac{1}{1000}$

$0.004 = \dfrac{4}{1000} = \dfrac{1}{250}$

$2.004 = 2\dfrac{4}{1000} = 2\dfrac{1}{250}$

In the same way,

$0.027 = \dfrac{27}{1000}$

$3.027 = 3\dfrac{27}{1000}$

$0.215 = \dfrac{215}{1000} = \dfrac{43}{200}$

$6.215 = 6\dfrac{215}{1000} = 6\dfrac{43}{200}$

 **Let's Practise!**

3 Convert each decimal to a fraction or mixed number. Write in the simplest form where possible.

a   6.7

b   12.5

c   7.08

d   5.51

e   0.075

f   2.179

g   1.035

h   6.004

Let's Learn!

Multiplying by tens, hundreds and thousands

Multiplying by 10

1 **a** Starting from 0, Ella takes steps of 0·1 on the number line. Where will she be after 10 steps?

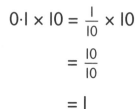

$$0.1 \times 10 = \frac{1}{10} \times 10$$

$$= \frac{10}{10}$$

$$= 1$$

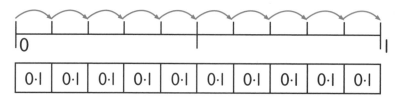

$3 \times 2 = 2 \times 3$
So
$10 \times 0.1 = 0.1 \times 10$.

$1 \text{ tenth} = 0.1 = \frac{1}{10}$

Ella will be at 1 on the number line.

b Starting from 0, Jack takes steps of 0·11 on the number line. Where will he be after 10 steps?

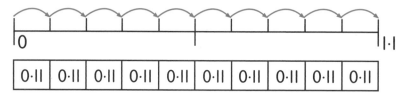

$$0.11 \times 10 = \frac{11}{100} \times 10$$

$$= \frac{11}{10}$$

$$= 1\frac{1}{10}$$

$$= 1.1$$

Jack will be at 1·1 on the number line.

c Starting from 0, Millie takes steps of 0·111 on the number line. Where will she be after 10 steps?

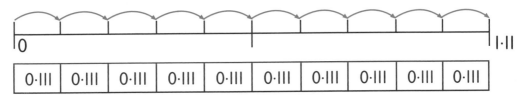

| 0·111 | 0·111 | 0·111 | 0·111 | 0·111 | 0·111 | 0·111 | 0·111 | 0·111 | 0·111 |

$$0·111 \times 10 = \frac{111}{100\cancel{0}} \times \cancel{1}0$$

$$= \frac{111}{100} = 1\frac{11}{100}$$

$$= 1·11$$

Millie will be at 1·11 on the number line.

2 Write each decimal as a fraction and then multiply. Give your answer as a decimal where necessary.

a $0·7 \times 10 = \dfrac{\Box}{\Box} \times 10 = \bigcirc$

b $0·07 \times 10 = \dfrac{\Box}{\Box} \times 10 = \bigcirc$

c $0·23 \times 10 = \bigcirc$

d $0·023 \times 10 = \bigcirc$

e $0·004 \times 10 = \bigcirc$

f $0·404 \times 10 = \bigcirc$

3

$$1 \times 10 = 10 \qquad\qquad 0 \cdot 1 \times 10 = 1$$
$$11 \times 10 = 110 \qquad\quad 0 \cdot 11 \times 10 = 1 \cdot 1$$
$$111 \times 10 = 1110 \qquad 0 \cdot 111 \times 10 = 1 \cdot 11$$

Now look at the chart below.

	Hundreds	Tens	Ones	•	Tenths	Hundredths
Number		1	1			
11 × 10	1	1	0			
Number			1			
1 × 10		1	0			
Number			0		1	
0·1 × 10			1			
Number			0		1	1
0·11 × 10			1		1	

In each case, what happens to the digits in the number when we multiply the number by 10?

Here is another example.

> Each digit moves 1 place to the left in the place value chart.

	Tens	Ones	•	Tenths	Hundredths	Thousandths
Number		5		9	2	8
5·928 × 10	5	9		2	8	

$5 \cdot 928 \times 10 = 59 \cdot 28$

Activity

4 Copy the chart below and complete it. An example is shown.

	Hundreds	Tens	Ones	•	Tenths	Hundredths	Thousandths
16·8		1	6		8		
16·8 × 10	1	6	8				
1·68			1		6	8	
1·68 × 10							
0·168			0		1	6	8
0·168 × 10							

What answers did you get?

16·8 × 10 = ⬭

1·68 × 10 = ⬭

0·168 × 10 = ⬭

We can also get the answers in this way.

1 6·8 × 10 = ⬭

1·6 8 × 10 = ⬭

0·1 6 8 × 10 = ⬭

When multiplying a decimal by 10, there is a short cut to get the answer.

Just shift the decimal point 1 place to the right.

a   5·9 × 10 = 59

b   5·9 2 8 × 10 = 59·28

5 Find the value of each of the following:

a   4·5 × 10 = ⬭

b   0·56 × 10 = ⬭

c   12·6 × 10 = ⬭

d   0·027 × 10 = ⬭

e   3·08 × 10 = ⬭

f   5·078 × 10 = ⬭

6 Find the missing numbers.

   a $0.03 \times \boxed{} = 0.3$ **b** $57.3 \times \boxed{} = 573$

   c $\boxed{} \times 10 = 264.7$ **d** $10 \times \boxed{} = 81.45$

Multiplying by tens

7 $3 \times 20 = 60$

$$\begin{array}{r} 2\ 0 \\ \times \quad 3 \\ \hline 6\ 0 \\ \hline \end{array}$$

We can also work out the product like this:

$$\begin{aligned} 3 \times 20 &= 3 \times 2 \times 10 \\ &= 6 \times 10 \\ &= 60 \end{aligned}$$

In the same way

$$\begin{aligned} 0.3 \times 20 &= 0.3 \times 2 \times 10 \\ &= 0.6 \times 10 \\ &= 6 \end{aligned}$$

and

$$\begin{aligned} 0.03 \times 20 &= 0.03 \times 2 \times 10 \\ &= 0.06 \times 10 \\ &= 0.6 \end{aligned}$$

8 What are the missing numbers?

   a $\begin{aligned} 4 \times 30 &= 4 \times \boxed{} \times 10 \\ &= \boxed{} \times 10 \\ &= \boxed{} \end{aligned}$ **b** $\begin{aligned} 0.4 \times 30 &= 0.4 \times \boxed{} \times 10 \\ &= \boxed{} \times 10 \\ &= \boxed{} \end{aligned}$

   c $\begin{aligned} 0.04 \times 30 &= 0.04 \times 3 \times \boxed{} \\ &= \boxed{} \times 10 \\ &= \boxed{} \end{aligned}$ **d** $\begin{aligned} 0.004 \times 30 &= 0.004 \times \boxed{} \times \boxed{} \\ &= \boxed{} \times \boxed{} \\ &= \boxed{} \end{aligned}$

> **Home Maths**   Ask your child to show how to multiply a decimal by 10 by:
> (1) moving the digits   (2) shifting the decimal point.

Multiplying by 100 and 1000

9 Look at these examples.

a **i** $0.3 \times 100 = \frac{3}{10} \times 100$
$= 3 \times 10 = 30$

ii $0.3 \times 1000 = \frac{3}{10} \times 1000$
$= 3 \times 100 = 300$

b **i** $0.03 \times 100 = \frac{3}{100} \times 100$
$= 3$

ii $0.03 \times 1000 = \frac{3}{100} \times 1000$
$= 3 \times 10 = 30$

c **i** $0.003 \times 100 = \frac{3}{1000} \times 100$
$= \frac{3}{10} = 0.3$

ii $0.003 \times 1000 = \frac{3}{1000} \times 1000$
$= 3$

10 Write each decimal as a fraction and then multiply. Give your answer as a decimal where necessary.

a $0.09 \times 100 = \dfrac{\square}{\square} \times 100$
$= \square$

b $0.9 \times 100 = \square$

c $0.18 \times 100 = \square$

d $0.018 \times 100 = \square$

e $0.066 \times 1000 = \dfrac{\square}{\square} \times 1000$
$= \square$

f $0.06 \times 1000 = \square$

g $0.117 \times 1000 = \square$

h $0.017 \times 1000 = \square$

9

II Look at the chart below.

	Thousands	Hundreds	Tens	Ones	·	Tenths	Hundredths	Thousandths
Number				3				
3 × 100		3	0	0				
3 × 1000	3	0	0	0				
Number				0		0	0	3
0.003 × 100		0	0	0		3		
0.003 × 1000	0	0	0	3				

000·3 is 0·3 and 0003 is 3.

What do you observe about the digits of a number when we multiply it by 100 and by 1000?

Here are other examples.

	Thousands	Hundreds	Tens	Ones	·	Tenths	Hundredths	Thousandths
Number				8		5	4	9
8·549 × 100		8	5	4		9		
8·549 × 1000	8	5	4	9				

8·549 × 100 = 854·9

8·549 × 1000 = 8549

Activity

12 Copy the chart below and complete it. An example is shown.

	Thousands	Hundreds	Tens	Ones	•	Tenths	Hundredths	Thousandths
12·03			1	2		0	3	
12·03 × 100	1	2	0	3				
3·009				3		0	0	9
3·009 × 100								
4·19				4		1	9	
4·19 × 1000								
0·013				0		0	1	3
0·013 × 1000								

What answers did you get?

12·03 × 100 = ☐

3·009 × 100 = ☐

4·19 × 1000 = ☐

0·013 × 1000 = ☐

We can also get the answers in this way.

1 2·0 3 × 100 = ☐

3·0 0 9 × 100 = ☐

4 ·1 9 × 1000 = ☐

0 · 0 1 3 × 1000 = ☐

Activity

When multiplying a decimal by 100, there is a short cut to get the answer.

Just shift the decimal point 2 places to the right.

a 8·5 4 9 × 100 = 854·9   **b** 8·5 × 100 = 850

c 8·5 4 9 × 1000 = 8549

d 8·5 4 × 1000 = 8540

So when multiplying a decimal by 1000, just shift the decimal point 3 places to the right.

13 Find the value of each of the following:

a 2·9 × 100 = ⬚   **b** 3·09 × 100 = ⬚

c 1·259 × 100 = ⬚   **d** 4·7 × 1000 = ⬚

e 4·75 × 1000 = ⬚   **f** 0·475 × 1000 = ⬚

14 Find the missing numbers.

a 3·1 × ⬚ = 310   **b** 5·029 × ⬚ = 502·9

c 14·03 × ⬚ = 14 030   **d** ⬚ × 0·045 = 45

e ⬚ × 100 = 23   **f** 1000 × ⬚ = 1302

Home Maths Ask your child to show how to multiply a decimal by 100 and 1000 by:
(1) moving the digits   (2) shifting the decimal point.

Multiplying by hundreds and thousands

15 Multiply **a** 0·8 by 200 and **b** 0·14 by 3000.

a $0·8 × 200 = 0·8 × 2 × 100$
$= 1·6 × 100$
$= 160$

b $0·14 × 3000 = 0·14 × 3 × 1000$
$= 0·42 × 1000$
$= 420$

16 What are the missing numbers?

a $0·7 × 400 = 0·7 × \boxed{} × 100$
$= \boxed{} × 100$
$= \boxed{}$

b $0·19 × 4000 = 0·19 × 4 × \boxed{}$
$= \boxed{} × 1000$
$= \boxed{}$

c $0·143 × 3000 = 0·143 × \boxed{} × 1000$
$= \boxed{} × 1000$
$= \boxed{}$

Activity

17 Work in pairs.

a Use a ruler to measure your handspan in centimetres correct to 1 decimal place. Find the length of:

i 10 of your handspans in centimetres

ii 50 of your handspans in centimetres.

b Use a metre rule to measure your pace in metres correct to 2 decimal places. Find how far you would have walked if you had taken:

i 100 paces **ii** 1000 paces.

Give your answer in metres.

I pace

13

Let's Practise!

18 Copy and complete the table below.

Number	24·5	3·54	0·136	2·079	42·05
Number × 10	⬭	⬭	⬭	⬭	⬭
Number × 100	⬭	⬭	⬭	⬭	⬭
Number × 1000	⬭	⬭	⬭	⬭	⬭

19 Find the value of each of the following:

   a $0·5 \times 30$ **b** $1·5 \times 50$ **c** $0·04 \times 40$

   d $0·44 \times 60$ **e** $0·027 \times 70$ **f** $0·127 \times 80$

20 Find the value of each of the following:

   a $0·2 \times 300$ **b** $1·6 \times 400$ **c** $2·6 \times 500$

   d $0·24 \times 600$ **e** $2·36 \times 700$ **f** $0·018 \times 800$

21 Find the value of each of the following:

   a $0·3 \times 2000$ **b** $8·7 \times 3000$ **c** $0·46 \times 6000$

   d $1·05 \times 4000$ **e** $0·021 \times 7000$ **f** $2·019 \times 5000$

22 Find the missing numbers.

> **Example**
>
> $168·9 = 16·89 \times 10 = 1·689 \times 100$

   a $35·6 = 3·56 \times \boxed{} = 0·356 \times \boxed{}$

   b $58 = 5·8 \times \boxed{} = 0·58 \times \boxed{} = 0·058 \times \boxed{}$

   c $2365 = \boxed{} \times 10 = \boxed{} \times 100 = \boxed{} \times 1000$

Practice Book 5B, p.1

Let's Learn!

Dividing by tens, hundreds and thousands

Dividing by 10

 a Starting from 1, Peter takes 10 equal steps backwards on the number line and lands on the point 0. What is the length of each step?

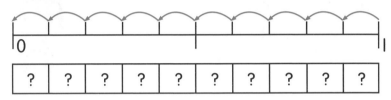

$$1 \div 10 = 1 \times \frac{1}{10}$$

$$= \frac{1}{10}$$

$$= 0{\cdot}1$$

The length of each step is **0·1**.

b Starting from 0·1, Ruby takes 10 equal steps backwards on the number line and lands on the point 0. What is the length of each step?

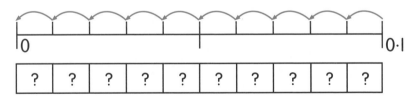

$$0{\cdot}1 \div 10 = \frac{1}{10} \div 10$$

$$= \frac{1}{10} \times \frac{1}{10}$$

$$= \frac{1}{100}$$

$$= 0{\cdot}01$$

The length of each step is **0·01**.

c Starting from 0·11, Omar takes 10 equal steps backwards on the number line and lands on the point 0. What is the length of each step?

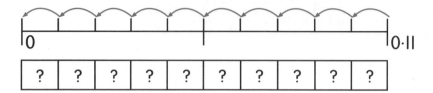

$$0{\cdot}11 \div 10 = \frac{11}{100} \div 10$$

$$= \frac{11}{100} \times \frac{1}{10}$$

$$= \frac{11}{1000}$$

$$= 0{\cdot}011$$

The length of each step is **0·011**.

2 Divide. Give your answer as a decimal.

a $3 \div 10 = \boxed{}$ **b** $17 \div 10 = \boxed{}$

c $307 \div 10 = \boxed{}$ **d** $3017 \div 10 = \boxed{}$

3 Write each decimal as a fraction and divide. Give your answer as a decimal.

a $0{\cdot}3 \div 10 = \boxed{}$ **b** $0{\cdot}31 \div 10 = \boxed{}$

c $0{\cdot}17 \div 10 = \boxed{}$ **d** $0{\cdot}07 \div 10 = \boxed{}$

4 Look at the chart below.

	Hundreds	Tens	Ones	•	Tenths	Hundredths
Number	I	I	0			
110 ÷ 10		I	I		0	
Number		I	0			
10 ÷ 10			I		0	
Number			I			
1 ÷ 10			0		I	
Number			0		I	
0·1 ÷ 10			0		0	I

11·0 is 11 and 1·0 is 1.

In each case, what happens to the digits in the number when we divide the number by 10?

Each digit moves I place to the right in the place value chart.

Here is another example.

	Hundreds	Tens	Ones	•	Tenths	Hundredths	Thousandths
Number		4	3		0	7	
43·07 ÷ 10			4		3	0	7

43·07 ÷ 10 = 4·307

Activity

5 Copy the chart below and complete it. An example is shown.

	Hundreds	Tens	Ones •	Tenths	Hundredths	Thousandths
163	1	6	3			
163 ÷ 10		1	6	3		
72·6		7	2	6		
72·6 ÷ 10						
0·29			0	2	9	
0·29 ÷ 10						

What answers did you get?

163 ÷ 10 = ⬚

72·6 ÷ 10 = ⬚

0·29 ÷ 10 = ⬚

We can also get the answers by shifting the decimal point.

1 6‿3 ÷ 10 = ⬚

7‿2·6 ÷ 10 = ⬚

‿0·2 9 ÷ 10 = ⬚

When dividing a number by 10, there is a short cut to get the answer.

Just shift the decimal point 1 place to the left.

a 4 3‿·0 7 ÷ 10 = 4·307   **b** 4 3‿·7 ÷ 10 = 4·37

6 Find the value of each of the following:

a $291 \div 10 = \boxed{}$

b $49 \cdot 1 \div 10 = \boxed{}$

c $6 \cdot 31 \div 10 = \boxed{}$

d $4 \cdot 07 \div 10 = \boxed{}$

e $6 \cdot 78 \div 10 = \boxed{}$

f $89 \cdot 02 \div 10 = \boxed{}$

g $45 \cdot 6 \div \boxed{} = 4 \cdot 56$

h $0 \cdot 55 \div \boxed{} = 0 \cdot 055$

i $\boxed{} \div 10 = 39 \cdot 14$

j $\boxed{} \div 10 = 1 \cdot 008$

Dividing by tens

7 $60 \div 20 = \dfrac{60}{20} = 3$

We can also work out the quotient like this:

$$60 \div 20 = 60 \div 2 \div 10$$
$$= 30 \div 10$$
$$= 3$$

In the same way $\quad 6 \div 20 = 6 \div 2 \div 10$
$$= 3 \div 10$$
$$= 0 \cdot 3$$

$$0 \cdot 6 \div 20 = 0 \cdot 6 \div 2 \div 10$$
$$= 0 \cdot 3 \div 10$$
$$= 0 \cdot 03$$

and $\quad 0 \cdot 06 \div 20 = 0 \cdot 06 \div 2 \div 10$
$$= 0 \cdot 03 \div 10$$
$$= 0 \cdot 003$$

Home Maths Ask your child to show how to divide a decimal by 10 by:
(1) moving the digits (2) shifting the decimal point.

8 What are the missing numbers?

a $8 \div 40 = 8 \div \boxed{} \div 10$

$ = \boxed{} \div 10$

$ = \boxed{}$

b $0{\cdot}8 \div 40 = 0{\cdot}8 \div \boxed{} \div 10$

$\phantom{0{\cdot}8 \div 40} = \boxed{} \div 10$

$\phantom{0{\cdot}8 \div 40} = \boxed{}$

c $0{\cdot}08 \div 40 = 0{\cdot}08 \div 4 \div \boxed{}$

$\phantom{0{\cdot}08 \div 40} = \boxed{} \div 10$

$\phantom{0{\cdot}08 \div 40} = \boxed{}$

Dividing by 100 and 1000

9 Look at these examples.

a $30 \div 100 = \dfrac{3\cancel{0}}{10\cancel{0}}$

$ = \dfrac{3}{10}$

$ = 0{\cdot}3$

b $3 \div 100 = \dfrac{3}{100}$

$ = 0{\cdot}03$

c $0{\cdot}3 \div 100 = \dfrac{3}{10} \div 100$

$\phantom{0{\cdot}3 \div 100} = \dfrac{3}{10} \times \dfrac{1}{100}$

$\phantom{0{\cdot}3 \div 100} = \dfrac{3}{1000}$

$\phantom{0{\cdot}3 \div 100} = 0{\cdot}003$

d $300 \div 1000 = \dfrac{30\cancel{0}}{100\cancel{0}}$

$ = \dfrac{3}{10}$

$ = 0{\cdot}3$

e $30 \div 1000 = \dfrac{3\cancel{0}}{100\cancel{0}}$

$ = \dfrac{3}{100}$

$ = 0{\cdot}03$

f $3 \div 1000 = \dfrac{3}{1000}$

$ = 0{\cdot}003$

10 Divide. Use the method shown in **9**.

a $70 \div 100 = \boxed{}$

b $7 \div 100 = \boxed{}$

c $0{\cdot}7 \div 100 = \boxed{}$

d $7{\cdot}7 \div 100 = \boxed{}$

e $900 \div 1000 = \boxed{}$

f $90 \div 1000 = \boxed{}$

g $99 \div 1000 = \boxed{}$

h $9 \div 1000 = \boxed{}$

11 Look at this chart.

	Thousands	Hundreds	Tens	Ones	• Tenths	Hundredths	Thousandths
Number	3	0	0	0			
3000 ÷ 100			3	0	0	0	
3000 ÷ 1000				3	0	0	0
Number				3			
3 ÷ 100				0	0	3	
3 ÷ 1000				0	0	0	3

30·00 is 30 and 3·000 is 3.

When we divide a number by 100, each digit in the number moves 2 places to the right in the place value chart.

So when we divide a number by 1000, each digit in the number moves 3 places to the right in the place value chart.

Here are other examples.

	Thousands	Hundreds	Tens	Ones	• Tenths	Hundredths	Thousandths
Number	4	0	7	1			
4071 ÷ 100			4	0	7	1	
4071 ÷ 1000				4	0	7	1

4071 ÷ 100 = 40·71
4071 ÷ 1000 = 4·071

Activity

12 Copy the chart below and complete it. An example is shown.

	Thousands	Hundreds	Tens	Ones •	Tenths	Hundredths	Thousandths
235		2	3	5			
235 ÷ 100				2	3	5	
53·2			5	3	2		
53·2 ÷ 100							
64			6	4			
64 ÷ 1000							
4061	4	0	6	1			
4061 ÷ 1000							

What answers did you get?

235 ÷ 100 = ☐

53·2 ÷ 100 = ☐

64 ÷ 1000 = ☐

4061 ÷ 1000 = ☐

We can also get the answers by shifting the decimal point.

2 3 5 ÷ 100 = ☐

5 3·2 ÷ 100 = ☐

6 4 ÷ 1000 = ☐

4 0 6 1 ÷ 1000 = ☐

Activity

When dividing a decimal by 100, there is a short cut to get the answer.

Just shift the decimal point 2 places to the left.

a 4 0·7 ÷ 100 = 0·407   **b** 4 0 7 ÷ 100 = 4·07

So when dividing a decimal by 1000, just shift the decimal point 3 places to the left.

c 4 0 7 1 ÷ 1000 = 4·071

13 Find the value of each of the following:

a 308 ÷ 100 = ☐   **b** 3·8 ÷ 100 = ☐

c 30·8 ÷ 100 = ☐   **d** 2016 ÷ 1000 = ☐

e 201 ÷ 1000 = ☐   **f** 26 ÷ 1000 = ☐

14 Find the missing numbers.

a 420 ÷ ☐ = 4·2   **b** 70·5 ÷ ☐ = 0·705

c 1061 ÷ ☐ = 1·061   **d** 890 ÷ ☐ = 0·89

e ☐ ÷ 100 = 3·01   **f** ☐ ÷ 1000 = 67·25

Home Maths Ask your child to show how to divide a decimal by 100 and 1000 by:
(1) moving the digits   (2) shifting the decimal point.

23

Dividing by hundreds and thousands

15 Divide **a** 28 by 200 and **b** 69 by 3000.

a $28 \div 200 = 28 \div 2 \div 100$
$= 14 \div 100$
$= 0.14$

b $69 \div 3000 = 69 \div 3 \div 1000$
$= 23 \div 1000$
$= 0.023$

16 What are the missing numbers?

a $16 \div 400 = 16 \div \boxed{} \div 100$
$= \boxed{} \div 100$
$= \boxed{}$

b $36 \div 4000 = 36 \div \boxed{} \div 1000$
$= \boxed{} \div 1000$
$= \boxed{}$

Let's Explore!

17 Look at these three calculations:

a $9 \times 7 = 63$

b $0.9 \times 7 = \frac{9}{10} \times 7$
$= \frac{63}{10}$
$= 6.3$

c $0.09 \times 7 = \frac{9}{100} \times 7$
$= \frac{63}{10}$
$= 0.63$

Given that $23 \times 8 = 184$, answer these questions without further workings:

i 2.3×8

ii 0.23×8

Let's Practise!

18 Copy and complete the table below.

Number	4078	407	47·8	4·7	4·78
Number ÷ 10					

Number	4078	407·8	407	47·8	4·7
Number ÷ 100					

Number	4078	4780	4070	408	480
Number ÷ 1000					

19 Find, as a decimal, the value of each of the following:

a 18 ÷ 30   **b** 1·6 ÷ 40   **c** 24 ÷ 60

d 2·05 ÷ 50   **e** 0·14 ÷ 70   **f** 1·68 ÷ 80

20 Find the value of each of the following:

a 93 ÷ 300   **b** 19·2 ÷ 600   **c** 49·7 ÷ 700

d 164 ÷ 2000   **e** 75 ÷ 5000   **f** 2164 ÷ 4000

21 Find the missing numbers.

Example

0·23 = 2·3 ÷ 10 = 23 ÷ 100 = 230 ÷ 1000

a 0·68 = 6·8 ÷ ☐ = 68 ÷ ☐ = 680 ÷ ☐

b 3·72 = 37·2 ÷ ☐ = 372 ÷ ☐ = 3720 ÷ ☐

c 4·165 = ☐ ÷ 10 = ☐ ÷ 100 = ☐ ÷ 1000

Practice Book 5B, p.5

Let's Learn!

Using a calculator

Get to know your calculator

1 Follow the steps to type in decimals on your calculator.

Turn on the calculator.

	Display
	0

To type in 50·78, press: [5] [0] [·] [7] [8]

To type in £125·50, press: [1] [2] [5] [·] [5] [0]

Display
50.78
125.50

Activity

2 Work in pairs.

Type in these decimals on your calculator. Clear the display on your calculator before typing in the next decimal.

a   7·031   **b**   536·5

c   £28·65   **d**   £1090·25

Check the numbers displayed on your calculator with those of your partner.
Do you both get the same numbers on the display screen?

3 **a**   Add 23·06 and 8·799.

Press	Display
[C]	0
[2][3][·][0][6]	23.06
[+][8][·][7][9][9]	8.799
[=]	31.859

The answer is 31·859.

b Find the sum of £1275·50 and £876·75.

Remember to write the correct unit in your answer.

Press	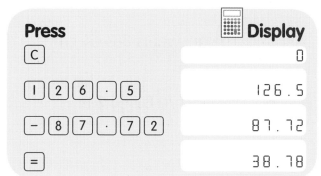 Display
C	0
1 2 7 5 . 5 0	1275.50
+ 8 7 6 . 7 5	876.75
=	2152.25

The sum of £1275·50 and £876·75 is £2152·25.

4 a Subtract 87·72 from 126·5.

Press	Display
C	0
1 2 6 . 5	126.5
− 8 7 . 7 2	87.72
=	38.78

The answer is 38·78.

b Find the difference between 10·05 kg and 240·8 kg.

Remember to write **kg** in your answer.

Press	Display
C	0
2 4 0 . 8	240.8
− 1 0 . 0 5	10.05
=	230.75

The difference between 10·05 kg and 240·8 kg is 230·75 kg.

Activity

5 ☷ Work in pairs to answer these questions.

a   176·07 + 28·94   **b**   656·8 m + 93·74 m

c   102·1 – 4·063   **d**   £325·60 – £65·05

Check your answers with those of your partner.

6 **a**   Find the area of a rectangle 36 cm long and 24·57 cm wide.

Press	Display
C	0
3 6	36
× 2 4 · 5 7	24.57
=	884.52

The answer is 884·52 cm².

b   Multiply 70·8 ℓ by 29.

Press	Display
C	0
7 0 · 8	70.8
× 2 9	29
=	2053.2

The answer is 2053·2 ℓ.

Remember to write ℓ in your answer.

7 **a** Divide 5·688 by 18.

Press	 Display
C	0
5 · 6 8 8	5.688
÷ 1 8	18
=	0.316

The answer is 0·316.

b Find 375·25 g ÷ 25.

> Remember to write g in your answer.

Press	Display
C	0
3 7 5 · 2 5	375.25
÷ 2 5	25
=	15.01

The answer is 15·01 g.

Activity

8 Work in pairs to answer these questions.

a 6·043 × 34   **b** 42 cm × 25·8 cm

c 4·875 ÷ 15   **d** £1436·50 ÷ 26

Check your answers with those of your partner.

Practice Book 5B, p.11

Let's Learn!

Word problems

1 Thirteen 5p coins are placed in a row touching one another as shown. Each coin measures 1·8 cm across. What is the total length of the row of coins?

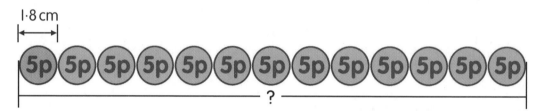

1·8 cm

5p 5p 5p 5p 5p 5p 5p 5p 5p 5p 5p 5p 5p

?

Total length of the row of coins

= 13 × 1·8

= 23·4

The total length of the row of coins is 23·4 cm.

Press	Display
C	0
1 3	13
× 1 · 8	1.8
=	23.4

Estimate 13 × 1·8 to check if the answer is reasonable.

13 × 1·8 ≈ 10 × 2
= 20
23·4 cm seems like a reasonable answer.

You can also check your answer by working backwards. Use your calculator to work out 23·4 ÷ 13. What value should you get?

I should get 1·8.

2  The mass of a 5p coin is about 3·25 g. Find the total mass of ninety-six 5p coins.

Total mass = ⬭ ◯ ⬭

= ⬭ g

The total mass of the coins is ⬭ g.

Estimate 96 × 3·25 to check if your answer is reasonable. How would you check your answer using your calculator?

3 A length of material 6·5 m long is cut into 2 pieces. One piece is twice as long as the other. What is the length of the longer piece? Give your answer to 2 decimal places.

longer piece [|]
shorter piece [   ]
} 6·5 m

The model above helps us to see that:

3 units ⟶ 6·5 m
1 unit ⟶ 6·5 ÷ 3 ≈ 2·167 m
2 units ⟶ 2 × 2·167 = 4·334 m
≈ 4·33 m

The length of the longer piece is about 4·33 m.

Press	Display
C	0
6 · 5	6.5
÷ 3 =	2.16666...

C	0
2 · 1 6 7	2.167
× 2	2
=	4.334

I can estimate to check the answer.
4·33 ≈ 4
4 ÷ 2 × 3 = 6 ≈ 6·5
So 4·33 m is reasonable.

4 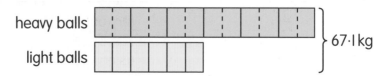 A sports shop has 6 light bowling balls and 6 heavy bowling balls. The mass of a heavy ball is twice that of a light ball. The total mass of the 12 balls is 67·1 kg. Find the total mass of the 6 heavy balls correct to the nearest kilogram.

heavy balls

light balls

67·1 kg

The model above helps us to see that:

◯ units ⟶ ◯ kg

1 unit ⟶ ◯ ◯ ◯ ≈ ◯ kg

12 units ⟶ ◯ ◯ ◯ = ◯ kg

≈ ◯ kg

The total mass of the 6 heavy balls correct to the nearest kilogram is about ◯ kg.

Activity

5 Work in pairs.
Find a supermarket website that gives the prices of the items it sells. Pupil A will act as the customer and Pupil B as the sales assistant.

a The customer will pick 3 items and the number of each item they want to buy, like this:

> 600 g of grapes at 40p per 100 g
> 4 packets of tea at £2·29 per packet
> 900 g of salmon at £1·67 per 100 g

b The customer will estimate the total cost.

c The sales assistant will then work out on their calculator the total amount the customer has to pay. They will compare that with the estimate from the customer.

d Take turns to play.

Let's Practise!

Solve these word problems. Check your answer by working backwards. Show your workings clearly.

6 Carol measures a whiteboard with her handspan and finds that it is 28 handspans long. The length of her handspan is 18·4 cm. What is the length of the whiteboard?

7 A box of baked beans contains 24 tins. The mass of each tin of baked beans is 0·39 kg. Find the mass of the 24 tins of baked beans.

8 1 kg of fish cost £8·75 and 1 kg of lamb cost £9·45. A café owner bought 16 kg of fish and 24 kg of lamb. How much did he pay altogether?

9 The sum of two numbers is 70·4. One of the numbers is 19 times the other. What are the two numbers?

10 The area of a square is 49 cm². The area of a rectangle is 19·9 cm² greater than that of the square and its length is 12 cm. Find the width of the rectangle in cm, correct to 2 decimal places.

11 Mrs Thomas bought two bags of rice of the same kind. One bag cost £10·65 and the other cost £6·30. The total mass of rice in the two bags was 15 kg. What was the price of 1 kg of rice?

12 Miya's family ate a total of 42·5 kg of rice in January and February. Her family ate 5·3 kg more rice in February than in January. How many kilograms of rice did Miya's family eat in February?

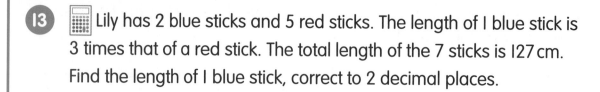

Let's Practise!

13 Lily has 2 blue sticks and 5 red sticks. The length of 1 blue stick is 3 times that of a red stick. The total length of the 7 sticks is 127 cm. Find the length of 1 blue stick, correct to 2 decimal places.

14 The perimeter of a rectangle is 45·8 cm. The perimeter of a square is 28·6 cm longer than that of the rectangle. Find the length of each side of the square.

15 Two buckets of different sizes contain 34·5 ℓ of water altogether. When 0·68 ℓ of water is poured from the bigger bucket into the smaller bucket, the amount of water in the bigger bucket is 9 times that in the smaller bucket. How much water was there in each bucket at first? Give your answer in litres.

Practice Book 5B, p.13

Let's Wrap It Up!

You have learnt to:

- convert decimals to fractions or mixed numbers
- multiply and divide a decimal by 10, 100 and 1000
- multiply and divide a decimal by tens, hundreds or thousands
- use estimation to check whether answers are reasonable.

Let's Wrap It Up!

Let's Revise!

The pupils of a primary school painted pieces of art paper for a school project. Each piece of paper has an area of $6 \cdot 25 \, cm^2$. The pupils painted 200 pieces in 1 day.

At the end of the second day, the pupils glued together all the pieces of paper side by side onto a large piece of cardboard. Then they cut the cardboard into 40 strips of equal sizes.

a What was the total area of the pieces of art paper that they had painted on both days?

Number of pieces painted in 2 days = 2 × 200 = 400
Total area = 6·25 × 400
$$= 6 \cdot 25 \times 4 \times 100$$
$$= 25 \times 100$$
$$= 2500 \, cm^2$$

The total area of the pieces of art paper they had painted was $2500 \, cm^2$.

b What was the area of each strip of cardboard? Give your answer as a mixed number.

$$\text{Area of each strip} = \frac{2500}{40}$$
$$= \frac{250}{4}$$
$$= \frac{125}{2}$$
$$= 62\frac{1}{2} \, cm^2$$

The area of each strip was $62\frac{1}{2} \, cm^2$.

Put On Your Thinking Caps!

Solve the following problems.

16 A sheet of soft plastic is 0·12 cm thick. The sheet of plastic is folded so that the folded sheet is twice as thick after each fold. How thick will it be after 4 folds? What is the least number of folds you have to make before the folded plastic is thicker than 3·6 cm?

17 Simone bought a total of 20 pastries and pies. Each pastry cost £1·50 and each pie cost £2·50. The pies cost £18 more than the pastries. How many of each item did she buy?

Practice Book 5B, p.20   Practice Book 5B, p.21

Unit 8 Measurements

Let's Learn!

> **Converting a measurement from a larger unit to a smaller unit**

Converting metres (m) to centimetres (cm)

1 Abby wants to cut out two pieces of ribbon 0·3 m and 1·05 m long. She has a 30 cm ruler. How can she measure the lengths of ribbon that she wants to cut?

Recall that:
1 m = 100 cm.

She can convert 0·3 m and 1·05 m to cm. She can then use her ruler to measure 30 cm and 105 cm.

$$0·3 \text{ m} = 0·3 \times 100 \text{ cm} = 30 \text{ cm}$$
$$1·05 \text{ m} = 1·05 \times 100 \text{ cm} = 105 \text{ cm}$$

2 Convert to centimetres (cm).

a $0.7 \text{ m} = 0.7 \times \boxed{} \text{ cm}$

$= \boxed{} \text{ cm}$

b $6·32 \text{ m} = 6·32 \times \boxed{} \text{ cm}$

$= \boxed{} \text{ cm}$

c $2·475 \text{ m} = 2·475 \times \boxed{} \text{ cm}$

$= \boxed{} \text{ cm}$

d $30·06 \text{ m} = 30·06 \times \boxed{} \text{ cm}$

$= \boxed{} \text{ cm}$

3 Express **a** 25·08 m   and   **b** 4·75 m in metres and centimetres.

a $0·08 \text{ m} = 0·08 \times 100 \text{ cm}$

$= 8 \text{ cm}$

$25·08 \text{ m} = 25 \text{ m } 8 \text{ cm}$

To express 25·08 m in m and cm, just convert 0·08 m to cm.

b $0.75\,m = 0.75 \times \boxed{}\,cm$

$= \boxed{}\,cm$

$4.75\,m = \boxed{}\,m\,\boxed{}\,cm$

4   Express in metres and centimetres.

a $15.09\,m$ **b** $112.6\,m$ **c** $62.08\,m$

Converting kilometres (km) to metres (m)

5   A car completes one lap of a racing track $4.35\,km$ in length. Find the distance covered in metres.

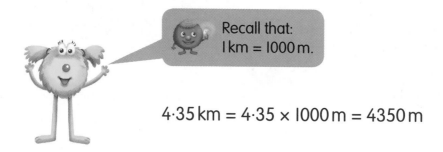

Recall that:
$1\,km = 1000\,m.$

$4.35\,km = 4.35 \times 1000\,m = 4350\,m$

6   Convert to metres (m).

a $30.5\,km = 30.5 \times \boxed{}\,m$ **b** $21.68\,km = 21.68 \times \boxed{}\,m$

$= \boxed{}\,m$ $= \boxed{}\,m$

c $0.125\,km = 0.125 \times \boxed{}\,m$ **d** $6.038\,km = 6.038 \times \boxed{}\,m$

$= \boxed{}\,m$ $= \boxed{}\,m$

7   Express **a** $16.55\,km$ and   **b** $9.074\,km$ in kilometres and metres.

a $0.55\,km = 0.55 \times 1000\,m$

$= 550\,m$

$16.55\,km = 16\,km\,550\,m$

To express $16.55\,km$ in km and m, just convert $0.55\,km$ to m.

b $0.074\,km = 0.074 \times$ ⬭ m

   $=$ ⬭ m

   $9.074\,km =$ ⬭ km ⬭ m

8 Express in kilometres and metres.

   a $19.2\,km$ **b** $4.035\,km$ **c** $23.58\,km$

Converting kilograms (kg) to grams (g)

9 The mass of a baby is $3.28\,kg$. What is the mass of the baby in grams?

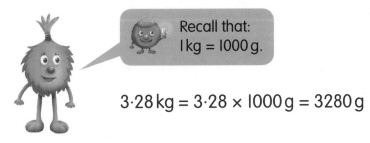

Recall that:
$1\,kg = 1000\,g.$

$3.28\,kg = 3.28 \times 1000\,g = 3280\,g$

10 Convert to grams (g).

   a $15.7\,kg = 15.7 \times$ ⬭ g   **b** $6.825\,kg = 6.825 \times$ ⬭ g

   $=$ ⬭ g $=$ ⬭ g

   c $80.04\,kg = 80.04 \times$ ⬭ g   **d** $244.6\,kg = 244.6 \times$ ⬭ g

   $=$ ⬭ g $=$ ⬭ g

11 Express **a** $8.605\,kg$ and   **b** $42.75\,kg$ in kilograms and grams.

   a $0.605\,kg = 0.605 \times 1000\,g$

   $= 605\,g$

   $8.605\,kg = 8\,kg\ 605\,g$

To express $8.605\,kg$ in kg and g, just convert $0.605\,kg$ to g.

39

b $0.75\,\text{kg} = 0.75 \times \boxed{}\,\text{g} = \boxed{}\,\text{g}$

  $42.75\,\text{kg} = \boxed{}\,\text{kg}\;\boxed{}\,\text{g}$

12 Express in kilograms and grams.

  a $100.4\,\text{kg}$ **b** $63.05\,\text{kg}$ **c** $9.088\,\text{kg}$

Activity

13 Work in pairs.
  a   Select three objects in your classroom that can be weighed.
  b   Use a weighing scale to find the masses of these three objects in kilograms correct to 1 decimal place.
  c   Convert each measurement to grams.
  d   Record your answers in a table like this.

Object			
Mass (kg)			
Mass (g)			

Converting litres (ℓ) to millilitres (ml)

14 A bottle of orange squash contains $1.25\,\ell$. Find its volume in millilitres.

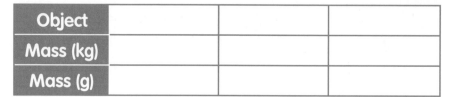

Recall that:
$1\,\ell = 1000\,\text{ml}$.

$1.25\,\ell = 1.25 \times 1000\,\text{ml} = 1250\,\text{ml}$

15 Convert to millilitres (ml).

  a $0.035\,\ell = 0.035 \times \boxed{}\,\text{ml}$ **b** $15.4\,\ell = 15.4 \times \boxed{}\,\text{ml}$

    $= \boxed{}\,\text{ml}$ $= \boxed{}\,\text{ml}$

  c $32.06\,\ell = 32.06 \times \boxed{}\,\text{ml}$ **d** $50.52\,\ell = 50.52 \times \boxed{}\,\text{ml}$

    $= \boxed{}\,\text{ml}$ $= \boxed{}\,\text{ml}$

16 Express **a** 8·028 ℓ   and   **b** 20·25 ℓ in litres and millilitres.

    a   0·028 ℓ = 0·028 × 1000 ml
                   = 28 ml
        8·028 ℓ = 8 ℓ 28 ml

To express 8·028 ℓ in ℓ and ml, just convert 0·028 ℓ to ml.

    b   0·25 ℓ = 0·25 × ☐ ml
               = ☐ ml
        20·25 ℓ = ☐ ℓ ☐ ml

17 Express in litres and millilitres.

    a   72·7 ℓ   **b**   11·03 ℓ   **c**   2·408 ℓ

Let's Practise!

18 Convert:
    a   0·2 m to centimetres   **b**   1·005 kg to grams
    c   10·07 ℓ to litres and millilitres **d**   30·09 m to metres and centimetres

19 2000 paper clips have a total mass of 6·5 kg. Find the total mass of 50 paper clips in grams.

20 Sound travels a distance of 19·88 km in 1 minute. How many metres does sound travel in 1 second? Give your answer correct to 1 decimal place.

21 Bella's family ate 5 kg of potatoes in a week. If her family ate the same mass of potatoes each day, how many grams of potatoes were eaten in 1 day? Give your answer correct to 1 decimal place.

22 Water flows from a tap at 5 ℓ per minute to fill a pot. It takes 9 seconds to fill the pot to the brim. Find the capacity of the pot in millilitres.

Practice Book 5B, p.23

Let's Learn!

Converting a measurement from a smaller unit to a larger unit

Converting centimetres (cm) to metres (m)

1 Mr Brook's handspan measures 23·5 cm. Express, as a decimal, his handspan in metres.

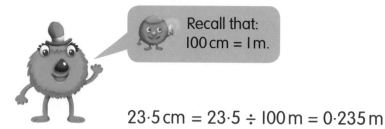

Recall that:
100 cm = 1 m.

$$23 \cdot 5 \, cm = 23 \cdot 5 \div 100 \, m = 0 \cdot 235 \, m$$

2 Express, as a decimal, in metres.

a $7 \, cm = 7 \div \boxed{} \, m$

        $= \boxed{} \, m$

b $280 \, cm = 280 \div \boxed{} \, m$

        $= \boxed{} \, m$

c $60 \cdot 8 \, cm = 60 \cdot 8 \div \boxed{} \, m$

        $= \boxed{} \, m$

d $123 \cdot 5 \, cm = 123 \cdot 5 \div \boxed{} \, m$

        $= \boxed{} \, m$

3 Express, as a decimal, in metres.

a   33 m 80 cm

b   200 m 5 cm

a $80 \, cm = \dfrac{80}{100} \, m = 0 \cdot 8 \, m$

      $33 \, m \, 80 \, cm = 33 \, m + 0 \cdot 8 \, m = 33 \cdot 8 \, m$

To express 33 m 80 cm as a decimal in m, just convert 80 cm to a decimal in m.

b $5 \, cm = \dfrac{5}{\boxed{}} = \boxed{} \, m$

      $200 \, m \, 5 \, cm = 200 \, m + \boxed{} \, m = \boxed{} \, m$

4 Express, as a decimal, in metres.

a   14 m 6 cm

b   105 m 40 cm

c   10 m 10 cm

Activity

5 Work in pairs.

a Select three objects in your classroom. Measure their lengths, heights and widths in centimetres correct to 1 decimal place.

b Convert each measurement to metres. Then record your answers in a table like this.

Object	Measurement in cm			Measurement in m		
	Length	Height	Width	Length	Height	Width

Converting metres (m) to kilometres (km)

6 The height of Mount Everest is about 8850 m. Express the height in km.

Recall that:
1000 m = 1 km.

$$8850\,m = \frac{8850}{1000}\,km = 8{\cdot}850\,km = 8{\cdot}85\,km$$

7 Convert to kilometres (km).

a 755 m = 755 ÷ ◯ km
= ◯ km

b 60 m = 60 ÷ ◯ km
= ◯ km

c 8970 m = 8970 ÷ ◯ km
= ◯ km

d 6005 m = 6005 ÷ ◯ km
= ◯ km

8 Express, as a decimal, in kilometres.

a 3 km 45 m

$$45\,m = \frac{45}{1000}\,km = 0{\cdot}045\,km$$
3 km 45 m = 3 km + 0·045 km
= 3·045 km

To express 3 km 45 m as a decimal in km, just convert 45 m to a decimal in km.

b   28 km 160 m

$$160 \, m = \frac{160}{\Box} km = \Box \, km$$

$$28 \, km \, 160 \, m = 28 \, km + \Box \, km$$
$$= \Box \, km$$

9   Express, as a decimal, in kilometres.

   a   3 km 315 m   **b**   2 km 8 m   **c**   275 km 700 m

Converting grams (g) to kilograms (kg)

10   A packet of rice has a mass of 2500 g. Find the mass in kilograms.

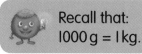

Recall that:
1000 g = 1 kg.

$$2500 \, g = \frac{2500}{1000} kg = 2.5 \, kg$$

11   Convert to kilograms (kg).

   a $50 \, g = 50 \div \Box \, kg$ **b** $3500 \, g = 3500 \div \Box \, kg$
   $\quad = \Box \, kg$ $\quad = \Box \, kg$

   c $4075 \, g = 4075 \div \Box \, kg$ **d** $6080 \, g = 6080 \div \Box \, kg$
   $\quad = \Box \, kg$ $\quad = \Box \, kg$

12   Express, as a decimal, in kilograms.

   a   350 kg 600 g

   $$600 \, g = \frac{600}{1000} kg = 0.6 \, kg$$
   $$350 \, kg \, 600 \, g = 350 \, kg + 0.6 \, kg$$
   $$= 350.6 \, kg$$

To express 350 kg 600 g as a decimal in kg, just convert 600 g to a decimal in kg.

b 78 kg 90 g

$$90\,g = 90 \div \boxed{} = \boxed{}\,kg$$

$$78\,kg\ 90\,g = \boxed{}\,kg$$

13 Express, as a decimal, in kilograms.

a 25 kg 460 g   **b** 20 kg 80 g   **c** 9 kg 5 g

Converting millilitres (ml) to litres (ℓ)

14 A bottle contains 750 ml of shampoo. Express the volume of shampoo in the bottle in litres.

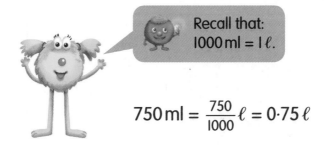

Recall that:
1000 ml = 1 ℓ.

$$750\,ml = \frac{750}{1000}\,\ell = 0{\cdot}75\,\ell$$

15 Convert to litres (ℓ).

a $75\,ml = 75 \div \boxed{}\,\ell$

$\qquad = \boxed{}\,\ell$

b $860\,ml = 860 \div \boxed{}\,\ell$

$\qquad = \boxed{}\,\ell$

c $15\,400\,ml = 15\,400 \div \boxed{}\,\ell$

$\qquad = \boxed{}\,\ell$

d $48\,060\,ml = 48\,060 \div \boxed{}\,\ell$

$\qquad = \boxed{}\,\ell$

16 Express, as a decimal, in litres.

a 2 ℓ 355 ml

$$355\,ml = \frac{355}{1000}\,\ell$$

$$= 0{\cdot}355\,\ell$$

$$2\,\ell\ 355\,ml = 2\,\ell + 0{\cdot}355\,\ell$$

$$= 2{\cdot}355\,\ell$$

To express 2 ℓ 355 ml in litres, just convert 355 ml to a decimal in ℓ.

b 50 ℓ 80 ml

$$80 \text{ml} = \frac{80}{\boxed{}} \ell = \boxed{} \ell$$

$$50 \ell \ 80 \text{ml} = 50 \ell + \boxed{} \ell = \boxed{} \ell$$

17 Express, as a decimal, in litres.

    a   85 ℓ 650 ml   **b**   60 ℓ 70 ml   **c**   755 ℓ 800 ml

18 15 handspans of Ella's dad measure 339 cm. How many metres will 2500 of his handspans measure?

15 handspans ⟶ 339 cm
1 handspan   ⟶ 339 ÷ 15
                 = 22·6 cm

2500 handspans ⟶ 2500 × 22·6
                     = 56 500 cm
                     = 56 500 ÷ 100
                     = 565 m

Press	Display
C	0
3 3 9	339
÷ 1 5	15
=	22.6
× 2 5 0 0	2500
=	56500
÷ 1 0 0	100
=	565

19 Farha's mum takes 20 paces to walk 13 m. How many kilometres has she walked after taking 12 000 paces?

20 paces   ⟶ 13 m
1 pace   ⟶ $\boxed{} \bigcirc \boxed{}$
          = $\boxed{}$ m
12 000 paces ⟶ $\boxed{} \bigcirc \boxed{}$
          = $\boxed{}$ m
          = $\boxed{} \bigcirc \boxed{}$ km
          = $\boxed{}$ km

Maths Journal

20 Ella converts metres to centimetres like this:

$$47 \cdot 5\,m = 47 \cdot 5 \div 100\,cm = 0 \cdot 475\,cm$$

Jack converts kilograms to grams like this:

$$4 \cdot 25\,kg = 4 \cdot 25 \times 100\,g = 425\,g$$

Explain what they did incorrectly.

21 Complete the statements below.

a To convert metres to centimetres, ⬚.

b To convert centimetres to metres, ⬚.

c To convert kilograms to grams, ⬚.

d To convert millilitres to litres, ⬚.

e To convert kilometres to metres, ⬚.

Home Maths   Ask your child to estimate the amount of water (in millilitres) they drink in a day. Then ask them to use their calculator to work out the amount they drink in a week, in a month, and in a year.

Let's Practise!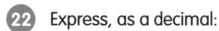

22 Express, as a decimal:
   a 170 cm in metres   **b** 2255 g in kilograms
   c 135 m 90 cm in metres   **d** 60 km 750 m in kilometres

Solve these word problems. Show your workings clearly.

23 Farha's mum drinks 6 cups of tea each day. Each cup contains 275 ml of tea. How many litres of tea does she drink in 1 week?

24 The adult human heart pumps about 5000 ml of blood in 1 minute. How many litres of blood does it pump in 1 day?

25 On a map, a length of 1 cm represents 30 000 cm on land. If a road measures 4·85 cm on a map, what is its actual length in metres?

> Practice Book 5B, p.29

Let's Wrap It Up!

You have learnt to:

- convert m to cm by multiplying by 100
- convert km to m, kg to g and ℓ to ml by multiplying by 1000
- convert cm to m by dividing by 100
- convert m to km, g to kg and ml to ℓ by dividing by 1000.

Let's Wrap It Up!

Let's Revise!

Convert:

a 1·075 m to cm

   1·075 m = 1·075 × 100 cm

          = 107·5 cm

b 304·7 kg to kg and g

   0·7 kg = 0·7 × 1000 g = 700 g

   304·7 kg = 304 kg 700 g

c 14 010 ml to ℓ

   14 010 ml = 14 010 ÷ 1000 ℓ

          = 14·01 ℓ

d 50 m 55 cm to m

   55 cm = 55 ÷ 100 m = 0·55 m

   50 m 55 cm = 50 + 0·55

              = 50·55 m

Put On Your Thinking Caps!

26 Estimate the number of cups of water you drink in a day. If a cup contains 325 ml of water, work out the amount of water (in litres) you would have drunk in 365 days.

27 A chef packs 10 kg of lentils into 750 g and 400 g packets. There are 2 more 400 g packets than 750 g packets. How many 750 g and 400 g packets did she pack?

Practice Book 5B, p.36 ▷   Practice Book 5B, p.37 ▷

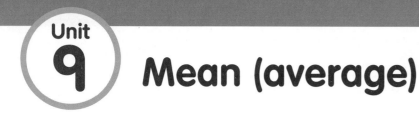

Unit 9 Mean (average)

Let's Learn!

Understanding mean (average)

1 Peter has 4 shells, Millie has 9 shells and Ruby has 8 shells. If all the shells are shared equally among the children, how many shells would each child get?

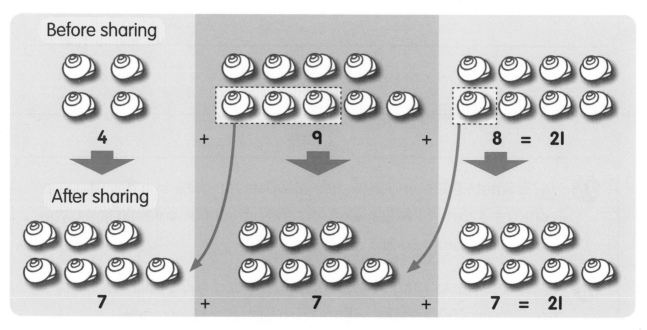

Before sharing

4 + 9 + 8 = 21

After sharing

7 + 7 + 7 = 21

Find the total number of shells.
4 + 9 + 8 = 21 shells
Then divide the total number of shells by the number of children.
21 ÷ 3 = 7 shells

Each child gets 7 shells.

$$\text{Mean number of shells} = \frac{\text{Total number of shells}}{\text{Number of children}}$$

The number of shells that each child will get if they are shared equally is 7.
7 is called the **mean**, or **average**, of 4, 9 and 8.

50

2 Tai, Miya, Hardeep and Omar sold stickers for charity. The table shows the number of stickers each person sold.

Tai	12
Miya	20
Hardeep	16
Omar	28

What is the mean number of stickers that each person sold?

Mean number of stickers sold = $\dfrac{\text{Total number of stickers sold}}{\text{Number of people}}$

Total number   12 + ⬭ + ⬭ + ⬭ = ⬭

Mean number   ⬭ ÷ ⬭ = ⬭ stickers

The mean number of stickers that each person sold is ⬭.

3 The following are the marks obtained by Farha, Jack and Chris in an English test.

Farha 53   Jack 84   Chris 46

a What is the total score obtained by Farha, Jack and Chris?

b What is their mean score?

a Total score = 53 + 84 + 46
= 183

The total score that Farha, Jack and Chris obtained is 183.

b Mean score = 183 ÷ 3
= 61

Their mean score is 61.

4 Mr Green walks 5 dogs whose masses are 28 kg, 34 kg, 56 kg, 42 kg and 60 kg.

    a   What is the dogs' total mass?

    b   What is their mean mass?

    a   Total mass = ◯ + ◯ + ◯ + ◯ + ◯

               = ◯ kg

        The dogs' total mass is ◯ kg.

    b   Mean mass = ◯ ÷ ◯

               = ◯ kg

        Their mean mass is ◯ kg.

$$\text{Mean} = \frac{\text{Total number or amount}}{\text{Number of items}}$$

5 Ella takes 4 tests in school. Her mean score for the 4 tests is 69 marks. What is her total score for the 4 tests?

Mean score for the 4 tests = 69
Number of tests she takes = 4

$$\frac{\text{Total}}{\text{score}} = \frac{\text{Mean}}{\text{score}} \times \frac{\text{Number of}}{\text{tests}}$$

Total score for the 4 tests = 69 × 4
                             = 276

Her total score for the 4 tests is 276.

6 Isabel spent all of her pocket money in 5 weeks. She spent a mean amount of £12·50 each week. How much did she spend altogether in 5 weeks?

Mean amount of money spent each week = £ ⬚

Number of weeks = ⬚

Total amount spent = £ ⬚ × ⬚

= £ ⬚

The total amount Isabel spent in 5 weeks was £ ⬚.

Activity

7 🖩 Work in groups of four.

Each person draws a red line and a blue line on a piece of paper. Use a ruler to measure the length of each person's lines. Record your answers in a table and answer the questions below.

Name				
Red line length				
Blue line length				

a Who drew the longest red line?

b Who drew the shortest red line?

c Who drew the longest blue line?

d Who drew the shortest blue line?

e The mean length of the red lines is ⬚ cm.

f The mean length of the blue lines is ⬚ cm.

Maths Journal

8 Look at the number sentences and pictures shown below. Then write a word problem based on the number sentences and the pictures.

a $300 \div 4 = 75$

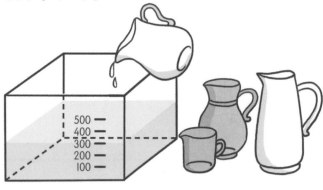

b $72 \times 3 = 216$

c $16 + 12 + 20 = 48$ $\qquad$ $48 \div 3 = 16$

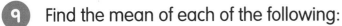

Let's Practise!

9 Find the mean of each of the following:

    a   4, 6, 10, 12 and 18   **b**   15, 25 and 32

    c   4, 8, 10, 13, 16 and 21   **d**   1·1, 2·2, 3·3, 4·4 and 5·5

10 For each of the following, find the mean.

    a   £4, £8, £5, £28 and £35   **b**   12ℓ, 26ℓ, 18ℓ, 27ℓ and 42ℓ

    c   38m, 46m, 72m and 85m   **d**   4·8kg, 6·6kg, 9·8kg and 14·2kg

11 In 4 matches, a netball team scored a total of 224 points. What was the team's mean score in the 4 matches?

12 Mark's scores for each basketball match he played were recorded below.

Match	First	Second	Third	Fourth	Fifth
Score	12	8	6	4	0

    a   What was the total score for the 5 matches Mark played?

    b   What was Mark's mean score for the 5 matches?

13 Maria buys 18 rolls of ribbon. The mean length of each roll of ribbon is 22·5m. Find the total length of all the rolls of ribbon.

14 The total mass of 22 bricks is 52·8kg. Find the mean mass of a brick.

15 Simon fills up 13 bottles with apple juice. There is a mean of 1075ml of apple juice in each bottle. What is the total volume of apple juice in the 13 bottles? Give your answer in litres and millilitres.

Practice Book 5B, p.49

55

Let's Learn!

Word problems

1 The mean mass of 2 dogs is 16 kg. The mass of one of the dogs is 12 kg. What is the mass of the other dog?

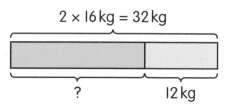

$2 \times 16\,kg = 32\,kg$

?   12 kg

Total mass of the 2 dogs = 16 × 2

= 32 kg

The mass of the other dog = 32 − 12

= 20 kg

The mass of the other dog is 20 kg.

2 Mrs Marsh bought chicken, fish and prawns at a market. The mean mass of the 3 items was 6·5 kg. The mass of chicken was 8 kg and the mass of fish was 4 kg. What was the mass of prawns that Mrs Marsh bought?

Total mass of chicken, fish and prawns bought = ⬚ × ⬚

= ⬚ kg

Mass of chicken and fish bought = ⬚ + ⬚

= ⬚ kg

Mass of prawns bought = ⬚ − ⬚

= ⬚ kg

Mrs Marsh bought ⬚ kg of prawns.

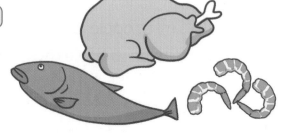

3 Kitty buys 20 books at a bookshop. The mean cost of 15 of the books is £11·50. The total cost of the other 5 books is £40·50. Find the mean cost of the 20 books.

Total cost of the 15 books = £11·50 × 15
= £172·50

Total cost of the 20 books = £172·50 + £40·50
= £213

Mean cost of the 20 books = £213 ÷ 20
= £10·65

The mean cost of the 20 books is £10·65.

4 Mr Smith owned a fleet of 11 trucks. The mean amount of petrol used per day by the first 7 trucks was 10·5 litres. The total amount of petrol used per day by the other 4 trucks was 28·8 litres. What was the mean amount of petrol used per day by all 11 trucks?

Amount of petrol used by the first 7 trucks = ☐ × ☐
= ☐ ℓ

Total amount of petrol used by all 11 trucks = ☐ + ☐
= ☐ ℓ

Mean amount of petrol used per day by all 11 trucks = ☐ ÷ ☐
= ☐ ℓ

The mean amount of petrol used per day by all 11 trucks was ☐ ℓ.

5 Some members of the Environment Club in Greenland Primary School took part in a waste paper collection project. The table below shows the mass of waste paper they collected. However, the total mass of waste paper collected by Group B was left out.

Group	Number of Members	Total Mass of Waste Paper Collected (kg)
A	4	9
B	5	?
C	9	23

a The mean mass of waste paper collected by each of the members in the three groups was 2·5 kg. Find the total mass of waste paper collected by Group B.

b What was the mean mass of waste paper collected by Group B?

a Total number of members in the three groups = 4 + ☐ + ☐

= ☐

Total mass collected by all the three groups = 2·5 × ☐

= ☐ kg

Total mass collected by Group B = ☐ − ☐ − ☐

= ☐ kg

The total mass of waste paper collected by Group B was ☐ kg.

b Mean mass collected by Group B = ☐ ÷ ☐

= ☐ kg

The mean mass of waste paper collected by Group B was ☐ kg.

6 The mean mass of a duck and a goose is 5 kg. The goose is 1·6 kg heavier than the duck. Find the mass of the goose.

Total mass of the duck and goose = 2 × 5 = 10 kg

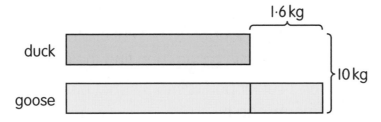

2 units ⟶ 10 − 1·6 = 8·4 kg

1 unit ⟶ 8·4 ÷ 2 = 4·2 kg

4·2 + 1·6 = 5·8 kg

The mass of the goose is 5·8 kg.

7 The mean height of a runner bean plant and a sunflower is 1·75 m. The runner bean plant is 0·3 m taller than the sunflower. How tall is the runner bean plant?

Total height = ☐ ◯ ☐ = ☐ m

sunflower

runner bean plant

☐ units ⟶ ☐ − ☐ = ☐ m

1 unit ⟶ ☐ m

☐ + 0·3 = ☐ m

The runner bean plant is ☐ m tall.

Let's Explore!

8 Take 3 strips of ribbon A, B and C, each 30 cm long.

   a Cut Ribbon A into 5 pieces of different lengths. Measure the lengths of the 5 pieces, then find their mean length.

   b Repeat this step for Ribbon B, but cut it into 5 pieces with lengths different from those in **a** and then find their mean length.

   c Measure and cut Ribbon C into 5 equal pieces. Find their mean length.

Compare the mean lengths in **a**, **b** and **c** above.
Are they different? Discuss your answer.

Let's Practise!

Solve these word problems. Show your workings clearly.

9 Mandy bought a mushroom pie and a chicken pie.
The mean cost of the 2 pies was £5·60.
The mushroom pie cost £4·65.

   a What was the total cost of the 2 pies?

   b How much did the chicken pie cost?

10 Chantal and 23 of her classmates drink water every morning. The mean volume of water each person drinks every morning is 750 ml. Chantal drinks 635 ml of water every morning.

   a What is the total volume of water Chantal and her classmates drink every morning?

   b What is the mean volume of water each of her 23 classmates drinks every morning?

Let's Practise!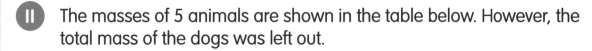

11 The masses of 5 animals are shown in the table below. However, the total mass of the dogs was left out.

	Animals	Total Mass
Dogs	Rex, Patch	?
Sheep	Fluffy, Lucky, Snowdrop	104 kg

The mean mass of the 5 animals is 32·8 kg.

a Find the total mass of the dogs.

b Find the mean mass of the dogs.

12  A shopkeeper bought 25 radios. The mean cost of 12 of the radios was £28. The total cost of the other 13 radios was £442.

a Find the total cost of the 25 radios.

b Find the mean cost of the 25 radios.

13 Ethan, Basha, Sian and Jacob took part in a quiz. Ethan and Basha's mean score was 78. Sian and Jacob's total score was 192. What was the 4 children's mean score?

14 The mean volume of juice in Jug A and Jug B is 1·65 ℓ. Jug A contains 0·4 ℓ of juice more than Jug B. Find the volume of juice in each jug.

15 Mr and Mrs Brown's mean salary is £2735·50. Mr Brown earns £233 less than Mrs Brown. How much does each of them earn?

Let's Practise!

16 Ahmed plays his favourite computer game every day. From Monday to Wednesday, his mean score was 580. From Thursday to Sunday, his mean score was 657. Find his total score from Monday to Sunday.

17 Liam bought 3 action figures at a mean cost of £12·40. The first action figure cost £0·80 more than the second action figure. The second action figure cost £0·40 less than the third action figure. What was the cost of the cheapest action figure?

18 Ava sold 4 times as many brownies as Bella at a school fair. Both of them sold a mean of 285 brownies. How many more brownies did Ava sell than Bella?

Practice Book 5B, p.55

Let's Wrap It Up!

You have learnt that:

- mean = $\dfrac{\text{Total number or amount}}{\text{Number of items}}$
- total number or amount = mean × number of items.

Let's Revise!

Mr Johnson bought 9 model cars at a toy fair. The mean cost of 4 of the model cars was £77·20 while the total cost of the remaining 5 model cars was £262·25.
Find the total cost of the 9 model cars. What is the mean cost of each model car?

Let's Wrap It Up!

Cost of first 4 model cars = £77·20 × 4 = £308·80
Therefore the total cost of 9 model cars = £308·80 + £262·25 = £571·05
Mean cost of each model car = £571·05 ÷ 9 = £63·45

The 9 model cars cost £571·05 altogether.
The mean cost of each model car is £63·45.

Put On Your Thinking Caps!

19 In a maths competition, Team A and Team B each has an equal number of children. The total number of children in each team is less than 10. The mean score of the children in Team A is 48 marks. The mean score of the children in Team B is 62 marks. The total score of Team B is 42 marks more than that of Team A.
Find the number of children in each team.

Practice Book 5B, p.61   Practice Book 5B, p.63

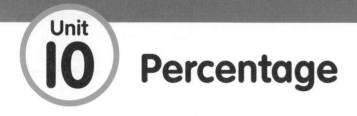

Unit 10 Percentage

Let's Learn!

Per cent

1

In a garden, there are 100 tulips.
75 of them are red.

So 75 out of 100 tulips are red.

There are three ways to express this.

> Compare the number of red tulips with the total number of tulips.
>
> $\dfrac{\text{Number of red tulips}}{\text{Total number of tulips}} = \dfrac{75}{100}$

As a Fraction	As a Decimal	As a Percentage
$\dfrac{75}{100}$	0·75	75%

> We read 75% as **75 per cent**.
> 75% means 75 out of 100.

2

The big square is divided into 100 equal parts.
25 parts are shaded.

So 25 out of 100 parts are shaded.

$\frac{25}{100}$ of the big square is shaded.

25% of the big square is shaded.

What percentage of the whole is shaded?
What percentage of the whole is not shaded?

3

⬜ % of the big square is shaded.

⬜ % of the big square is **not** shaded.

4 Express each of the following as a percentage.

a 72 out of 100 is ⬜ %.

b 39 out of 100 is ⬜ %.

5 Express each fraction as a percentage.

a $\dfrac{17}{100} = \boxed{}\%$

b $\dfrac{68}{100} = \boxed{}\%$

6 Express each fraction as a percentage.

a $\dfrac{7}{10} = \dfrac{70}{100} = \boxed{}\%$

b $\dfrac{3}{10} = \dfrac{\boxed{}}{100} = \boxed{}\%$

$\dfrac{7}{10} = \dfrac{70}{100}$

Find the equivalent fraction of $\dfrac{7}{10}$ that has 100 as its denominator.

7 Express each decimal as a percentage.

a $0{\cdot}45 = \dfrac{45}{100}$
$\phantom{0{\cdot}45} = 45\%$

b $0{\cdot}7 = 0{\cdot}70$
$\phantom{0{\cdot}7} = \dfrac{70}{100}$
$\phantom{0{\cdot}7} = 70\%$

c $0{\cdot}03 = \dfrac{3}{100}$
$\phantom{0{\cdot}03} = 3\%$

8 Express each decimal as a percentage.

a $0{\cdot}56 = \dfrac{\boxed{}}{100}$
$\phantom{0{\cdot}56} = \boxed{}\%$

b $0{\cdot}9 = \dfrac{\boxed{}}{10} = \dfrac{\boxed{}}{100}$
$\phantom{0{\cdot}9} = \boxed{}\%$

c $0{\cdot}4 = \dfrac{\boxed{}}{\boxed{}}$
$\phantom{0{\cdot}4} = \boxed{}\%$

d $0{\cdot}08 = \dfrac{\boxed{}}{\boxed{}}$
$\phantom{0{\cdot}08} = \boxed{}\%$

9 Express **a** 8% and **b** 64% as a fraction in its simplest form.

a $8\% = \dfrac{\cancel{8}^{\,2}}{\cancel{100}_{\,25}}$
$ = \dfrac{2}{25}$

b $64\% = \dfrac{\cancel{64}^{\,16}}{\cancel{100}_{\,25}}$
$ = \dfrac{16}{25}$

10 Express each percentage as a fraction in its simplest form.

a 94% = $\dfrac{\boxed{}}{100}$

   = $\dfrac{\boxed{}}{\boxed{}}$

b 88% = $\dfrac{\boxed{}}{100}$

   = $\dfrac{\boxed{}}{\boxed{}}$

c 42% = $\dfrac{\boxed{}}{\boxed{}}$

d 56% = $\dfrac{\boxed{}}{\boxed{}}$

e 12% = $\dfrac{\boxed{}}{\boxed{}}$

f 78% = $\dfrac{\boxed{}}{\boxed{}}$

g 34% = $\dfrac{\boxed{}}{\boxed{}}$

h 66% = $\dfrac{\boxed{}}{\boxed{}}$

11 Express **a** 48% and **b** 79% as a decimal.

a 48% = $\dfrac{48}{100}$

   = 0·48

b 79% = $\dfrac{79}{100}$

   = 0·79

Remember, when dividing a number by 100, just shift the decimal point 2 places to the left.

12 Express each percentage as a decimal.

a 38% = $\dfrac{\boxed{}}{100}$

   = $\boxed{}$

b 4% = $\dfrac{\boxed{}}{100}$

   = $\boxed{}$

c 97% = $\dfrac{\boxed{}}{100}$

   = $\boxed{}$

d 60% = $\dfrac{\boxed{}}{100}$

   = $\boxed{}$

Activity

13 Work in pairs.
Copy the diagram below and fill in the boxes. An example is shown.

Fraction	$\frac{7}{100}$	$\frac{22}{100}$	☐	☐
Decimal	0·07	☐	☐	0·75
Percentage	7%	☐	52%	☐

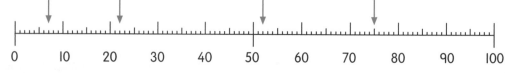

0   10   20   30   40   50   60   70   80   90   100

Let's Practise!

14 Express each fraction as a percentage.

a $\frac{42}{100}$ b $\frac{85}{100}$ c $\frac{9}{100}$

d $\frac{4}{100}$ e $\frac{4}{10}$ f $\frac{8}{10}$

15 Express each decimal as a percentage.

a 0·63   b 0·44   c 0·3

d 0·9   e 0·05   f 0·08

16 Express each percentage as a fraction in its simplest form.

a 23%   b 71%   c 2%

d 45%   e 76%   f 54%

Let's Practise!

17 Express each percentage as a decimal.

    a   24%   **b**   3%   **c**   17%

    d   70%   **e**   69%   **f**   33%

18 Write each of the following as a fraction in its simplest form and then as a percentage.

    a   11 out of 100   **b**   73 out of 100

    c   8 out of 100   **d**   9 out of 10

19 Express the shaded part of the whole as a percentage.

    a 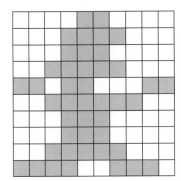   **b** 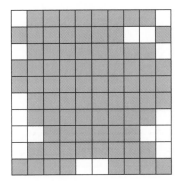

20 Of the 100 people who visited a museum last Wednesday, 63 were tourists.

    a   What percentage of the people who visited the museum were tourists?

    b   What percentage of the people who visited the museum were not tourists?

21 Mr Lowe collects 100 pieces of fruit from his garden. 34 of the pieces of fruit are apples and the rest are pears.

    a   What percentage of the pieces of fruit are apples?

    b   What percentage of the pieces of fruit are pears?

Let's Practise!

22 On a sheet of paper, copy the number line shown below. Write the following percentages on the number line.

| **a** 28% | **b** 49% | **c** 4% | **d** 77% |

0%   50%   100%

23 Express each percentage as a decimal. Copy the number line shown below, then mark the decimal on it.

| **a** 14% | **b** 55% | **c** 7% | **d** 98% |

0   0·5   1·0

Practice Book 5B, p.65

Maths Journal

24 Look at Emily's and Basha's answers to the questions below. Whose answer is correct? Explain your answer.

a Express $\frac{7}{10}$ as a percentage.

Emily's answer: 7%   Basha's answer: 70%

b Express 0·1 as a percentage.

Emily's answer: 1%   Basha's answer: 10%

c Express 54% as a fraction in its simplest form.

Emily's answer: $\frac{27}{50}$ Basha's answer: $\frac{27}{20}$

Let's Learn!

Converting more fractions to percentages

1 Emma spent $\frac{1}{4}$ of her money on a book. What percentage of her money did she spend on the book?

Method 1

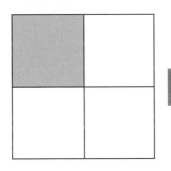 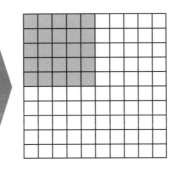

$$\frac{1}{4} = \frac{25}{100} = 25\%$$

First convert the denominator of the fraction to 100.
Multiply the numerator and denominator by 25.

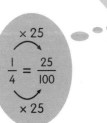

$$\frac{1}{4} = \frac{25}{100}$$
$$\times 25$$

Method 2

Whole	Spent
$1 = \frac{4}{4}$	$\frac{1}{4}$
100%	? %

There is more than one method to convert a fraction to a percentage.

A whole is $\frac{4}{4}$ or 100%.

1 whole → 100%

4 parts → 100%

1 part → $\frac{100}{4}\% = 25\%$

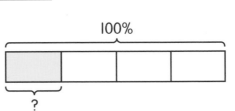

Method 3

$$\frac{1}{4} = \frac{1}{4} \times 100\% = 25\%$$

2 Use the models to express each fraction as a percentage.

a Express $\frac{3}{4}$ as a percentage.

4 parts ⟶ 100%

1 part ⟶ $\frac{\boxed{}}{\boxed{}}$% = $\boxed{}$%

3 parts ⟶ 3 × $\boxed{}$% = $\boxed{}$%

So $\frac{3}{4}$ = $\boxed{}$%.

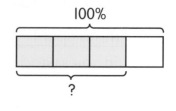

b Express $\frac{2}{5}$ as a percentage.

5 parts ⟶ 100%

1 part ⟶ $\boxed{}$%

2 parts ⟶ $\boxed{}$%

So $\frac{2}{5}$ = $\boxed{}$%.

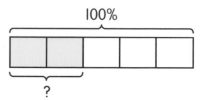

c Express $\frac{7}{8}$ as a percentage.

8 parts ⟶ $\boxed{}$%

1 part ⟶ $\frac{\boxed{}}{\boxed{}}$% = $\boxed{}$%

7 parts ⟶ 7 × $\boxed{}$% = $\boxed{}$%

So $\frac{7}{8}$ = $\boxed{}$%.

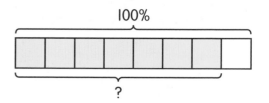

3 Express each fraction as a percentage.

a $\frac{3}{5} = \frac{\boxed{}}{100}$ **OR** $\frac{3}{5} = \frac{3}{5} \times \boxed{}$%

$\phantom{\frac{3}{5}} = \boxed{}$% $\phantom{\frac{3}{5}} = \boxed{}$%

b $\frac{7}{20} = \frac{\boxed{}}{100}$ **OR** $\frac{7}{20} = \frac{\boxed{}}{20} \times \boxed{}$%

$\phantom{\frac{7}{20}} = \boxed{}$% $\phantom{\frac{7}{20}} = \boxed{}$%

4 Mr Lee had 500 pineapples for sale. He sold 200 of them to Mr Simms.

    a What percentage of the pineapples were sold to Mr Simms?

    b What percentage of the pineapples were left?

    a Fraction of pineapples sold = $\frac{200}{500}$ = $\frac{2}{5}$

        Percentage of pineapples sold = $\frac{2}{5}$ × 100% = 40%

        40% of the pineapples were sold to Mr Simms.

    b Percentage of pineapples left = 100% − 40% = 60%

        60% of the pineapples were left.

5 🖩 A baker bought 250 kg of flour to make bread. She used 120 kg of flour to make bread on Monday and the rest on Tuesday.

    a What percentage of the flour was used on Monday?

    b What percentage of the flour was used on Tuesday?

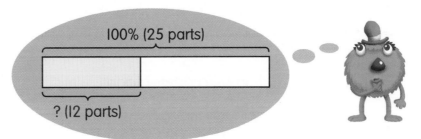

    a Fraction of flour used on Monday = $\frac{120}{250}$ = $\frac{12}{25}$

        Percentage of flour used on Monday = $\frac{12}{25}$ × 100%

                            = ⬚ %

        ⬚ of the flour was used on Monday.

    b Percentage of flour used on Tuesday = ⬚ % − ⬚ %

                            = ⬚ %

        ⬚ of the flour was used on Tuesday.

Activity

6 Work in pairs.

Set A

| 4 | 10 | 20 | 25 | 50 |

Set B

| 2 | 5 | 11 | 12 | 28 | 49 |

a Each pupil takes a turn to make a proper fraction by choosing the denominator from Set A and the numerator from Set B.

b Draw a model to show each fraction as a percentage.

c Pupils check each other's answers.

d The first pupil with the most number of correct models drawn wins.

Let's Practise!

7 Express each fraction as a percentage.

Example

$$\frac{4}{10} = \frac{40}{100} = 40\% \qquad \textbf{OR} \qquad \frac{4}{10} = \frac{4}{10} \times 100\% = 40\%$$

a $\frac{3}{20}$

b $\frac{24}{25}$

c $\frac{9}{50}$

d $\frac{4}{5}$

e $\frac{21}{50}$

f $\frac{17}{25}$

g $\frac{3}{10}$

h $\frac{13}{20}$

i $\frac{11}{25}$

Let's Practise!

8 Express each fraction as a percentage.

a $\dfrac{78}{200}$

b $\dfrac{260}{400}$

c $\dfrac{237}{300}$

d $\dfrac{135}{500}$

e $\dfrac{100}{625}$

f $\dfrac{21}{140}$

9 Express each fraction as a percentage. Round your answer to the nearest whole number.

a $\dfrac{89}{140}$

b $\dfrac{26}{235}$

c $\dfrac{150}{305}$

d $\dfrac{390}{468}$

e $\dfrac{13}{507}$

f $\dfrac{99}{101}$

10 At a cake shop, a baker sold $\dfrac{2}{5}$ of his cakes. What percentage of the cakes were sold?

11 Michael painted $\dfrac{13}{25}$ of a rectangular wall.

a What percentage of the wall was painted?

b What percentage of the wall was not painted?

12 At a school, $\dfrac{11}{25}$ of the pupils walk to school, $\dfrac{7}{20}$ travel by bus, while the rest travel by car.

a What percentage of pupils do not travel by car?

b What percentage of pupils travel by car?

Let's Practise!

Solve these word problems. Show your workings clearly.

13 A chef has 20 kg of pasta. She cooks 7 kg of it. What percentage of the pasta does the chef cook?

14 There are 900 pupils in a school. 540 of them are boys. What percentage of the pupils in the school are boys?

15 In a certain school, $\frac{3}{20}$ of the pupils cycle to school and the rest of the pupils do not.

   a What percentage of the pupils cycle to school?

   b What percentage of the pupils do not cycle to school?

16 Isabel's sister earns £800 a month. She gives £240 of it to her mum and keeps the rest.

   a What percentage of her money does she give to her mum?

   b What percentage of her money does she keep?

17 There are 250 seats on an aeroplane. 225 of the seats are in the economy class section, while the rest are in the first class section. $\frac{24}{25}$ of the seats in the economy class section are occupied.

   a What percentage of the seats are in the first class section?

   b What percentage of the seats in the economy class section are occupied?

18 There were 28 500 visitors to a theme park in a week. 17 100 of the visitors were adults. $\frac{13}{20}$ of the adults were men.

   a What percentage of the visitors were children?

   b What percentage of the total number of visitors were men?

Practice Book 5B, p.69

Let's Learn!

Percentage of a quantity

1 There were 400 seats on an aeroplane. 60% of the seats were in economy class. How many seats were in economy class?

Method 1

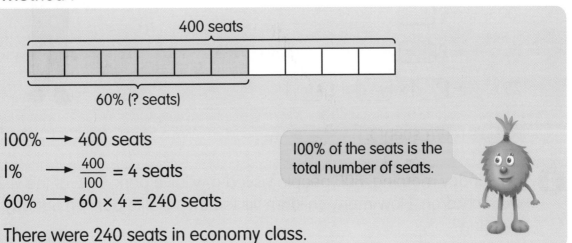

$100\%\longrightarrow 400$ seats

$1\%\longrightarrow \dfrac{400}{100}=4$ seats

$60\%\longrightarrow 60\times4=240$ seats

100% of the seats is the total number of seats.

There were 240 seats in economy class.

Method 2

60% of seats $= 60\%$ of 400

$\qquad = \dfrac{60}{1\cancel{00}}\times4\cancel{00}$

$\qquad = 60\times4$

$\qquad = 240$

There were 240 seats in economy class.

2 ▦ Farha's mum had £750. She spent 25% of her money. How much money did she spend?

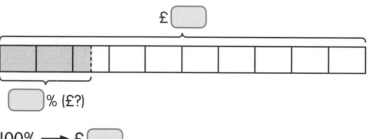

£ ⬡

⬡ % (£?)

100% ⟶ £ ⬡

1% ⟶ £ ⬡

25% ⟶ ⬡ × ⬡ = £ ⬡

Farha's mum spent £ ⬡ .

3 On Sunday morning, 800 people visited a wildlife park. 75% of the visitors were children. How many children visited the wildlife park on Sunday morning?

Total number of visitors = 800

75% of the visitors = 75% × ⬡

= ⬡

⬡ children visited the wildlife park on Sunday morning.

4 Mr Smith earns £2400 monthly. He spends 25% of the money on rent and 30% of the money on food.

a What percentage of his salary is left?

b How much money does he have left?

a

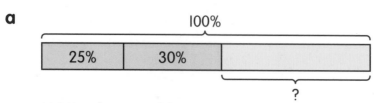

100% − 25% − 30% = 45%

45% of his salary is left.

b

£2400

| 55% | 45% |

?

Method I

100% → £2400

1% → $\frac{2400}{100}$ = £24

45% → 45 × £24 = £1080

Method 2

45% of £2400 = 45% × £2400

$= \frac{45}{100}$ × £2400

= 45 × £24

= £1080

Mr Smith has £1080 left.

5 Maria has 1200 apple, pear and peach trees altogether in her orchard. 20% of the trees are apple trees and 45% are pear trees. How many peach trees are there in the orchard?

100% – ⬡% – ⬡% = ⬡%

⬡% of Maria's trees are peach trees.

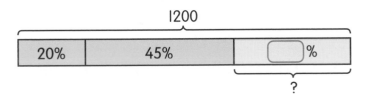

1200

| 20% | 45% | ⬡% |

?

Method I

100% → ⬡

1% → $\frac{\square}{\square}$ = ⬡

⬡% → ⬡ × ⬡ = ⬡

Method 2

⬡% of 1200 = ⬡% × 1200

$= \frac{\square}{100}$ × 1200

= ⬡ × ⬡

= ⬡

There are ⬡ peach trees in the orchard.

Activity

6 Work in pairs.
Draw models to show the following.

a A shopkeeper had 750 boxes of eggs. He sold 40% of the eggs.

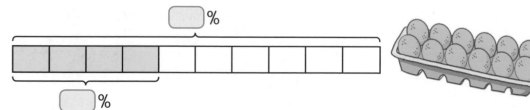

( )%

( )%

100% of the eggs = ( ) boxes

b Kerry has 450 ml of milk. She uses 75% of it to make pancakes.

c Mr Adams earns £720. He saves 25% of the money and spends the rest.

Maths Journal

7 Copy the model given below. Based on these number sentences and the model given:

1 write a word problem

2 complete the model

3 solve your word problem.

40% × 825 = 330   825 − 330 = 495

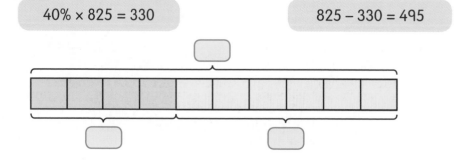

Let's Practise!

8 Find the value of:

    a $20\% \times 75$ **b** $30\% \times 80$

    c   45% of 720   **d**   62% of 550

Solve these word problems. Show your workings clearly.

9 A packet contained 560 g of flour. Rosa used 70% of it to make bread. How many grams of flour did she use to make bread?

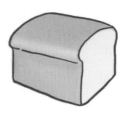

10 Sarah's weekly pocket money was £15. She spent 25% of her pocket money one week.

    a   How much money did she spend that week?

    b   How much money did she have left?

11 Last Saturday, 450 children took part in a fun run. 40% of them were boys. How many girls took part in the fun run?

12 Nick has a total of 200 chicken eggs and duck eggs. 75% of the eggs are chicken eggs. How many of the eggs are duck eggs?

Let's Practise!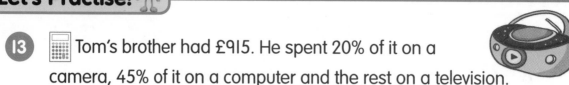

13 ▦ Tom's brother had £915. He spent 20% of it on a camera, 45% of it on a computer and the rest on a television.

 a What percentage of the money was spent on the television?

 b How much money was spent on the television?

14 A grocer bought 30 kg of fruit. 15% of the pieces of fruit were oranges and 60% of the pieces of fruit were apples. The rest were pears.

 a What percentage of the pieces of fruit bought were pears?

 b What was the mass of the pears that she bought?

15 An estate has 2500 residents. They live in bungalows, terrace houses or flats. 15% of the residents live in bungalows, 25% of the residents live in terrace houses and the rest live in flats.

 a What percentage of residents live in flats?

 b How many residents live in flats?

16 Sian bought 250 g of nuts. 22% of the nuts were almonds, 28% were hazelnuts and 44% were peanuts. The rest were cashews. She finished all the nuts except for the cashews.

 a What percentage of the nuts were cashews?

 b What was the mass of the nuts left?

Practice Book 5B, p.73

Let's Learn!

Word problems

1 Cheng's dad bought a television set that cost £1500. In addition, he insured it for 10% of the price.

a How much was the insurance?

b How much did Cheng's dad pay for the television set in total?

a   **Method 1**

£1500

10%

?

$100\% \longrightarrow £1500$

$1\% \longrightarrow \frac{1500}{100} = £15$

$10\% \longrightarrow 10 \times £15 = £150$

The insurance was £150.

Method 2

Insurance paid = 10% of £1500

$= \frac{10}{100} \times £1500$

$= £150$

The insurance was £150.

b   Total cost of the television set = £1500 + £150

= £1650

Cheng's dad paid £1650 in total for the television set.

2 Sophia's family went out for a meal. The cost of the food they ordered was £82. In addition, they paid a 15% service charge.

a How much was the service charge?

b How much did they pay for the meal in total?

a **Method 1**

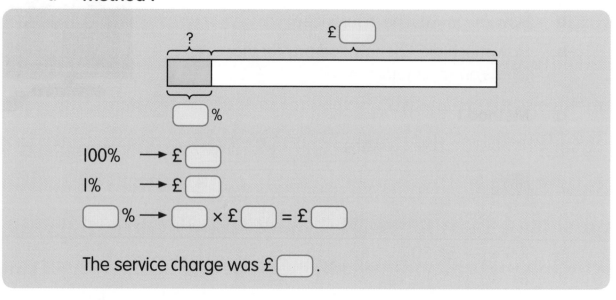

100% ⟶ £⬭

1% ⟶ £⬭

⬭% ⟶ ⬭ × £⬭ = £⬭

The service charge was £⬭.

Method 2

Service charge paid = ⬭% of £⬭

$$= \frac{\Box}{\Box} \times £\Box$$

$$= £\Box$$

The service charge was £⬭.

b Total cost of the meal = £⬭ + £⬭

$$= £\Box$$

They paid £⬭ in total for the meal.

3 The usual price of a computer was £2000. At a computer shop, Mrs White bought the computer and was given a 15% discount.

    a   How much was the discount given to Mrs White?

    b   How much did she pay for the computer in total?

    a   **Method 1**

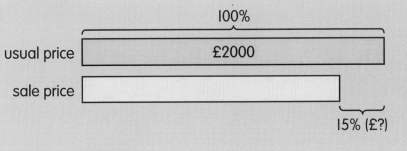

100% ⟶ £2000

1% ⟶ $\frac{2000}{100}$ = £20

15% ⟶ 15 × £20 = £300

The discount given to Mrs White was £300.

Method 2

Discount = 15% of usual price

        = $\frac{15}{100}$ × £2000

        = £300

The discount given to Mrs White was £300.

    b   Amount of money paid = £2000 – £300

                           = £1700

    Mrs White paid £1700 in total for the computer.

4 The usual price of a bicycle was £150. At a sale, Miss Williams bought the bicycle and was given a discount of 20%.

a How much was the discount?

b How much did she pay for the bicycle in total?

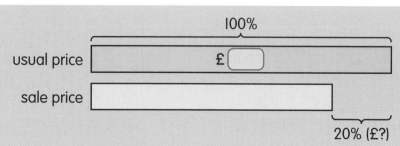

a **Method I**

100%

usual price [£ ⬚]

sale price [   ]

20% (£?)

100% ⟶ £⬚

1% ⟶ $\frac{⬚}{⬚}$ = £⬚

⬚% ⟶ ⬚ × £⬚ = £⬚

The discount was £⬚.

Method 2

Discount = ⬚% of £⬚

$= \frac{⬚}{⬚} × £⬚$

$= £⬚$

The discount was £⬚.

b Amount of money paid = £⬚ – £⬚

= £⬚

Miss Williams paid £⬚ in total for the bicycle.

5 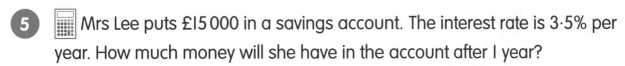 Mrs Lee puts £15 000 in a savings account. The interest rate is 3·5% per year. How much money will she have in the account after 1 year?

Interest = 3·5% of £15 000

$= \dfrac{3.5}{100} \times £15\,000$

= £525

> Add the interest to the amount invested.

Amount of money in the account after 1 year = £15 000 + £525
= £15 525

Mrs Lee will have £⬚ in the account after 1 year.

6 Mr Daniels has £200 000 in a savings account. The interest rate is 6% per year. How much money will he have in the account after 1 year?

Interest = ⬚% of £⬚

$= \dfrac{⬚}{⬚} \times £⬚$

= £⬚

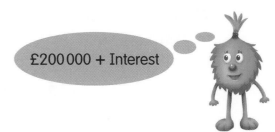

> £200 000 + Interest

Amount of money in the account after 1 year = £⬚ + £⬚
= £⬚

Mr Daniels will have £⬚ in the account after 1 year.

Activity

7 Work in pairs.
Draw models for each question. Label each model with the numbers provided in each question.

a Miss Brook bought a wardrobe which cost £149. She had to pay a delivery charge of 7% of £149. Draw a model to show the prices of the wardrobe before and after the delivery charge was included.

Activity

b The original price of a chair is £50. The shop owner increases the price by 30%. Draw a model to show the original price and new price of the chair.

c The usual price of a book was £16. The shop gave a discount of 10% on its usual price. Draw a model to show the usual price and discounted price of the book.

Maths Journal

8 The usual price of a table was £78. William's parents bought the table at a 5% discount. How much did they pay for the table? William, Ishani and Amos drew models to represent the word problem above.
Whose model is correct? Explain why.

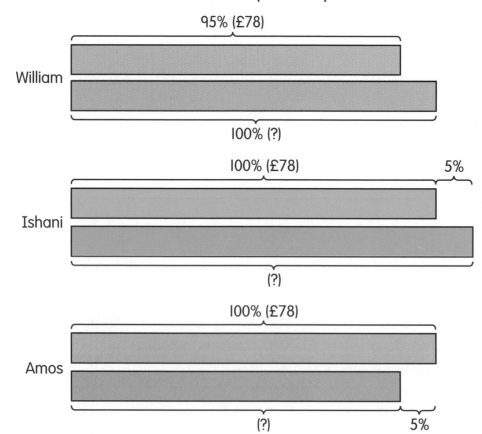

Let's Practise!

Solve these word problems. Show your workings clearly.

9 Mr Bell bought a sofa that cost £820. In addition, he had to pay a delivery charge of 5% on £820. How much delivery charge did Mr Bell pay?

10 Mrs Lee and her family had a meal that cost £90. In addition, they paid a 10% service charge.

    a How much service charge did they pay?

    b How much did they pay for the meal in total?

11 Mr Jackson bought a television set that cost £920. In addition, he insured it for 5% of the price. How much did he pay for the television set?

12 Mr Green went for dinner with his friends. The dinner cost £240. In addition, they paid a 15% tip. How much did they pay for the dinner in total?

13 The usual price of a computer was £650. Miss Thompson bought the computer and was given a discount of 5%. How much did Miss Thompson pay for the computer?

14 35 students went to a theme park. Each ticket cost £15 and they were each given a student discount of 15%. How much did they pay for the tickets in total?

15 Lucy's parents put £95 000 in a savings account. The interest rate is 5·5% per year. How much interest did they get after 1 year?

16 Sam's parents have put £185 000 in a savings account. The account has an interest rate of 6% per year. How much money will they have in the account after 1 year?

Practice Book 5B, p.77

89

Let's Wrap It Up!

You have learnt to:

- read the '%' symbol as 'per cent'
- express a part of a whole as a percentage
- express a fraction as a percentage
- express a decimal as a percentage
- express a percentage as a fraction in its simplest form or a decimal
- find the percentage of a given quantity
- solve word problems involving percentage, discount and annual interest.

Let's Revise!

140 children took part in a sports camp during the school holidays. 15% of the children were eligible for an 'Early Bird Discount'.

a What fraction of the children were eligible for the discount? Express your answer in its simplest form.

$$15\% = \frac{15}{100} = \frac{3}{20}$$

b How many children in the camp were not eligible for the discount?

Percentage of children that were not eligible = 100% − 15% = 85%

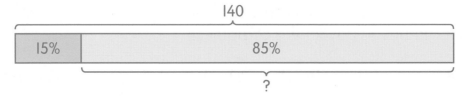

Method 1

100% $\longrightarrow$ 140

1% $\longrightarrow$ 140 ÷ 100 = 1·4

85% $\longrightarrow$ 85 × 1·4 = 119

Method 2

$$85\% \text{ of } 140 = \frac{85}{100} \times 140$$
$$= 119$$

119 children in the camp were not eligible for the discount.

Put On Your Thinking Caps!

17 In a school fund-raising project, 40% of the total amount collected was from the teachers. Parents and pupils contributed the remaining amount. The parents contributed twice as much as the pupils. What percentage of the total amount collected was contributed by the pupils?

Practice Book 5B, p.81 ▶   Practice Book 5B, p.82 ▶

Unit 11 Angles

Let's Learn!

Angles on a straight line

1 **a** QR is a straight line. ∠POQ and ∠POR are called angles on a straight line.

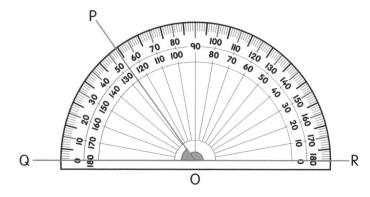

We can see that ∠POQ + ∠POR = 180°.

b SO is perpendicular to QR.

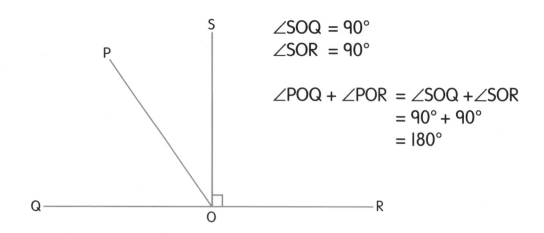

∠SOQ = 90°
∠SOR = 90°

∠POQ + ∠POR = ∠SOQ + ∠SOR
= 90° + 90°
= 180°

The sum of angles on a straight line is 180°.

Activity

2 AB is a straight line.

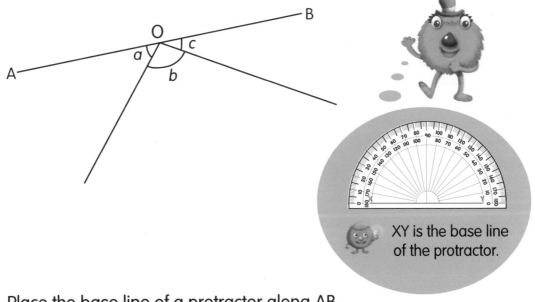

XY is the base line of the protractor.

Place the base line of a protractor along AB.
What can you say about ∠a + ∠b + ∠c?

∠a + ∠b + ∠c = ⬭

3 Measure the unknown marked angles.

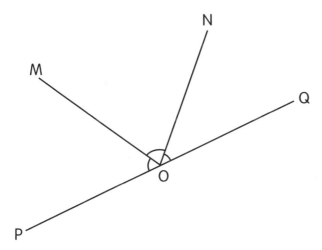

∠POM = ⬭
∠MON = ⬭
∠NOQ = ⬭

∠POM + ∠MON + ∠NOQ = ⬭

Are the three angles on a straight line?
Why?

4 Name the marked angles on the straight line XY and state the sum of the angles.

a

∠⬚ + ∠⬚ + ∠⬚

= ⬚

b

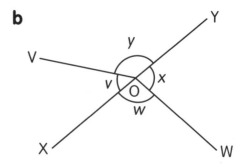

∠⬚ + ∠⬚ = ⬚

∠⬚ + ∠⬚ = ⬚

5 AC is a straight line. Find ∠x.

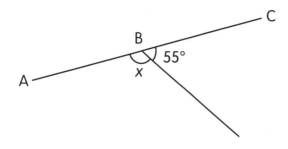

The sum of angles on a straight line is 180°.

∠x + 55° = 180°

So ∠x = 180° − 55°

= 125°.

6 XZ is a straight line. Find ∠y.

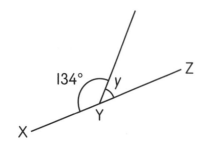

∠y = ⬚ − ⬚

= ⬚

Home Maths Encourage your child to measure ∠YOW, ∠WOV and ∠VOX in **4**a above using a protractor and confirm that their sum is 180°.

7 XZ is a straight line. Find ∠y.

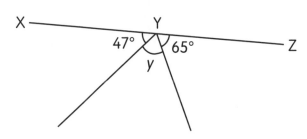

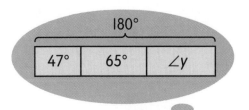

∠y + 47° + 65° = 180°

So ∠y = 180° − 47° − 65°
        = 68°.

8 AB is a straight line. Find ∠a.

∠a = ☐ − ☐ − ☐
   = ☐

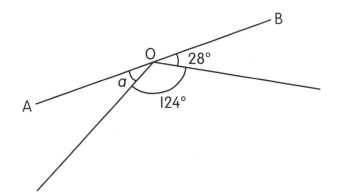

9 In each diagram, AB is a straight line. Find the unknown marked angle.

a

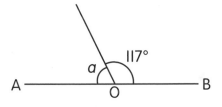

b

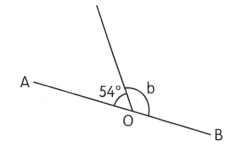

c

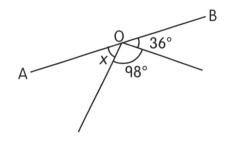

d

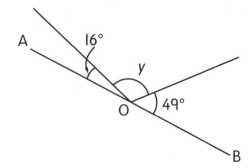

Activity

(10) Work in pairs.

a Check which of the sets of angles below can make angles on a straight line.

  i $\angle a = 98°$, $\angle b = 82°$

  ii $\angle p = 78°$, $\angle q = 35°$, $\angle r = 77°$

  iii $\angle w = 34°$, $\angle x = 29°$, $\angle y = 16°$, $\angle z = 101°$

b Write down a set of three angles which add up to 180°. Then write down another set of three angles which add up to more or less than 180°. Show each set of angles to your partner. Ask them to check which set can make angles on a straight line. Then ask them to draw these three angles on a straight line.

Maths Journal

(11) In the diagram, AB is a straight line and DO is perpendicular to AB. Explain why $\angle a + \angle b + \angle c = 180°$.

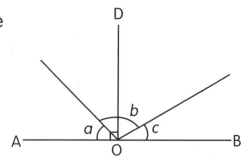

Practice Book 5B, p.91

Let's Learn!

Angles at a point

I AO, BO and CO are straight lines meeting at the point O.
∠a, ∠b and ∠c are known as angles at a point.

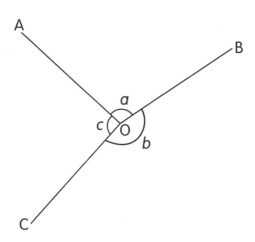

Extend the line AO to D.
AD is a straight line.

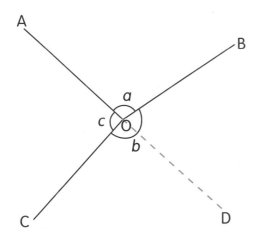

∠b = ∠BOD + ∠COD

∠a +   ∠b   + ∠c

= ∠a + ∠BOD + ∠COD + ∠c

$$= \underbrace{\angle a + \angle BOD}_{180°} + \underbrace{\angle COD + \angle c}_{180°}$$

= 360°

∠a and ∠BOD are angles on a straight line. ∠COD and ∠c are also angles on a straight line.

The sum of angles at a point is 360°.

2 ∠AOD, ∠DOC, ∠BOC and ∠AOB are angles made by four straight lines meeting at O. Measure the unknown marked angles and find the sum of the angles.

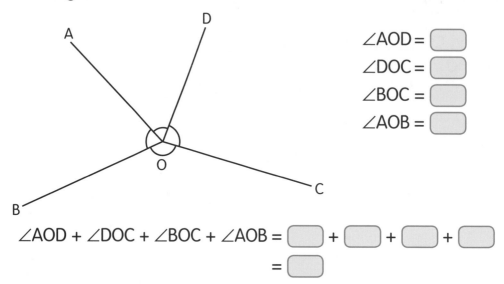

∠AOD = ⬚
∠DOC = ⬚
∠BOC = ⬚
∠AOB = ⬚

∠AOD + ∠DOC + ∠BOC + ∠AOB = ⬚ + ⬚ + ⬚ + ⬚

= ⬚

Are these angles at a point? Why?

Activity

3 XO, YO and ZO are straight lines meeting at the point O.
Place the base line of a protractor along XO as shown. Then make a $\frac{1}{2}$ turn of your protractor.

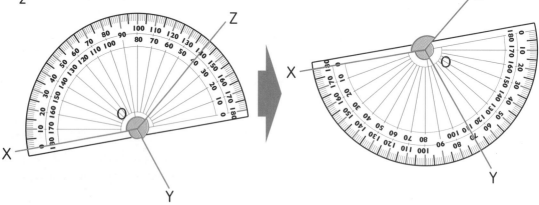

What can you say about ∠XOY + ∠YOZ + ∠ZOX?
∠XOY + ∠YOZ + ∠ZOX = ⬚ + ⬚

= ⬚

4 Name the angles at the point O and state the sum of the angles.

a

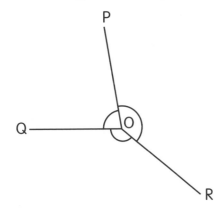

∠ ⬚ + ∠ ⬚ + ∠ ⬚
= ⬚

b

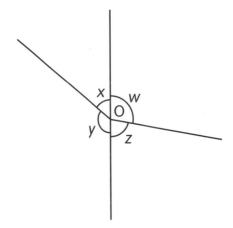

∠ ⬚ + ∠ ⬚ + ∠ ⬚ + ∠ ⬚
= ⬚

5 In the diagram, find ∠a.

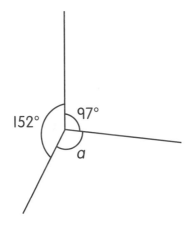

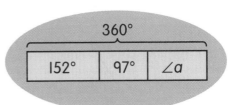

The sum of angles at a point is 360°.

$\angle a + 152° + 97° = 360°$

So $\angle a = 360° - 152° - 97°$
$= 111°$.

🏠 Home Maths — Encourage your child to measure ∠w, ∠x, ∠y and ∠z in **4b** above using a protractor and confirm that their sum is 360°.

6 The following diagram is not drawn to scale. Find ∠z.

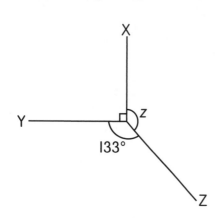

$$\angle z = \boxed{} - \boxed{} - \boxed{}$$
$$= \boxed{}$$

7 The following diagrams are not drawn to scale. Find the unknown marked angles.

a

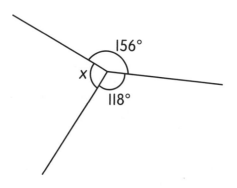

b

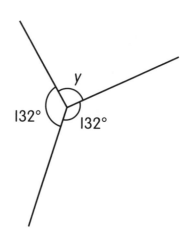

c

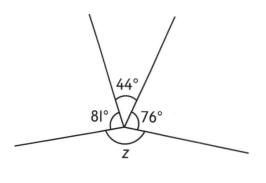

d

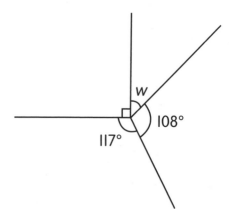

Activity

8 Work in pairs.

a Check which of the sets of angles below can make angles at a point.

　i　∠a = 87°, ∠b = 98°, ∠c = 175°

　ii　∠p = 36°, ∠q = 69°, ∠r = 107°, ∠s = 58°

　iii　∠w = 95°, ∠x = 48°, ∠y = 48°, ∠z = 169°

b Write down a set of four angles which add up to 360°. Then write down another set of four angles which add up to more or less than 360°.

Show each set of angles to your partner. Ask them to check which set can make angles at a point. Then ask them to draw these four angles meeting at a point.

Maths Journal

9 AB is a straight line.

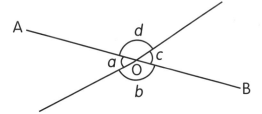

Explain why ∠a + ∠b + ∠c + ∠d = 360°.

Practice Book 5B, p.95

Let's Learn!

Vertically opposite angles

1 EF and GH are two straight lines which cross each other.

∠a and ∠c are called vertically opposite angles.
∠b and ∠d are also called vertically opposite angles.

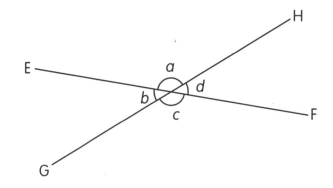

$\angle a + \angle b = 180°$
$\angle b + \angle c = 180°$
$\angle a + \angle b = \angle b + \angle c$

So $\angle a = \angle c$.

$\angle a + \angle b = 180°$
$\angle a + \angle d = 180°$
$\angle a + \angle b = \angle a + \angle d$

So $\angle b = \angle d$.

∠a and ∠b are angles on a straight line.
∠b and ∠c are also angles on a straight line.

∠a and ∠d are also angles on a straight line.

Vertically opposite angles are equal.

Activity

2   In the diagram, AB and CD are straight lines.

Copy the diagram below on a piece of tracing paper. Then fold the paper along the red dotted line.

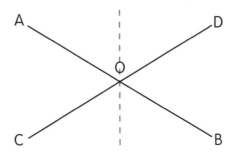

What can you conclude? ∠AOC = ∠⬭

Now fold the paper along the blue dotted line.

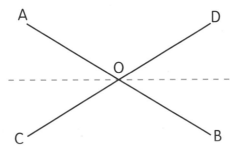

What can you conclude? ∠AOD = ∠⬭

3   The diagram shows the four angles made when two straight lines cross. Measure the unknown marked angles.

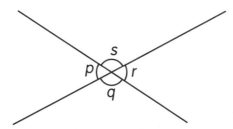

∠p = ⬭
∠q = ⬭
∠r = ⬭
∠s = ⬭

Which are the two pairs of vertically opposite angles? ⬭

---

4 In the diagram, PQ and RS are straight lines. Name the pairs of vertically opposite angles.

∠◻ and ∠◻ are vertically opposite angles.

∠◻ and ∠◻ are also vertically opposite angles.

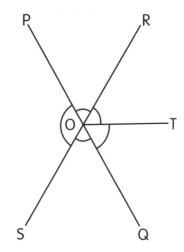

5 The following diagram is not drawn to scale. WX and YZ are straight lines. Find ∠WOY, ∠WOZ and ∠XOY.

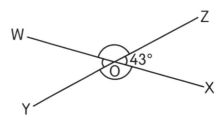

∠WOY = ∠ZOX
= 43°

∠WOZ + 43° = 180°
So ∠WOZ = 180° − 43°
= 137°.

∠XOY = ∠WOZ = 137°

Vertically opposite angles are equal.

The sum of angles on a straight line is 180°.

Home Maths — Encourage your child to measure ∠POR and ∠SOQ in **4** above and confirm that they are equal. Do the same with ∠POS and ∠ROQ.

6 The following diagram is not drawn to scale. PQ and RS are straight lines. TO is perpendicular to PQ. Find ∠x.

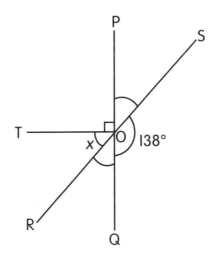

∠POR and ∠SOQ are vertically opposite angles.

∠x + ⬭ = ⬭

∠x = ⬭ – ⬭

= ⬭

7 The following diagrams are not drawn to scale. AB and CD are straight lines. Find the unknown marked angles.

a

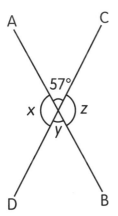

b

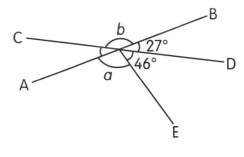

Activity

8 Measure the angles below.

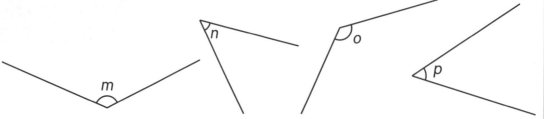

a Can this set of angles make 2 straight lines? Why?

b Draw the four angles meeting at a point so that

    i ∠m and ∠o   **ii** ∠p and ∠n

make vertically opposite angles.

9 Measure the angles in each set.

Set A

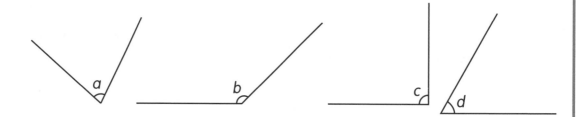

Set B

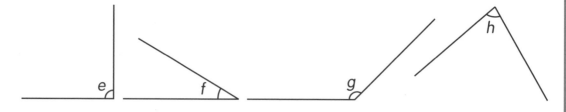

Which set of angles can be drawn to make angles at a point? Why?

Practice Book 5B, p.99

Maths Journal

10 AB and CD are straight lines.

Write three sentences on how
∠a, ∠b, ∠c and ∠d are related.

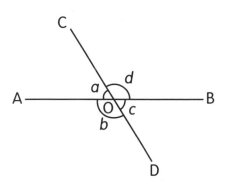

Let's Practise!

11 For each diagram, identify which of these are angles on a straight line, angles at a point and vertically opposite angles. Then copy and complete the table below. An example (A) is shown.

A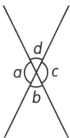

B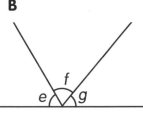

C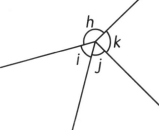

D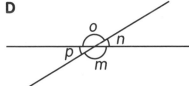

E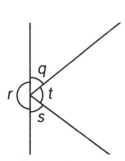

F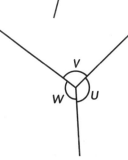

Diagram	Vertically Opposite Angles	Angles on a Straight Line	Angles at a Point
A	∠a and ∠c ∠b and ∠d	∠a and ∠b ∠c and ∠d ☐ ☐	∠a, ∠b, ∠c and ∠d

Let's Practise!

12 What is the sum of angles on a straight line?

13 What is the sum of angles at a point?

14 Can angles of 70°, 45° and 65° make angles on a straight line?
Explain your answer.

15 Can angles of 10°, 90°, 45° and 45° make angles on a straight line?
Explain your answer.

16 **a** Can angles of 50°, 50°, 130° and 130° make angles at a point?
Explain your answer.

 b Can the angles in **a** also make vertically opposite angles?
Explain your answer.

The following diagrams are not drawn to scale. Find the unknown marked
angles in each of them.

17 AB is a straight line.
Find ∠a.

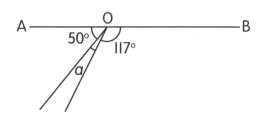

18 MN is a straight line.
Find ∠c and ∠d.

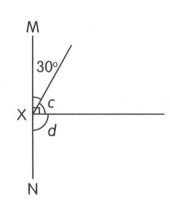

Let's Practise!

19 Find ∠e.

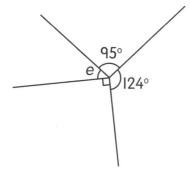

20 PQ and RS are straight lines.
Find ∠POR and ∠ROQ.

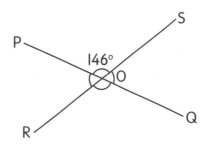

21 AB is a straight line.
Find ∠h and ∠i.

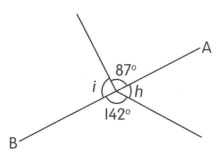

22 Find ∠m.

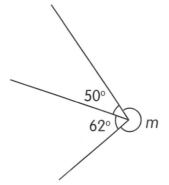

23 Find ∠n.

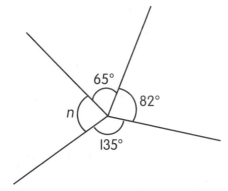

Let's Practise!

24 AB and CD are straight lines.
Find ∠j and ∠k.

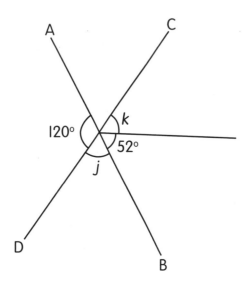

25 AB is a straight line.
∠a = ∠b. Find ∠a.

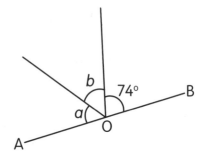

26 MN, PQ and RS are
straight lines.
Find the sum of ∠b, ∠d and ∠f.

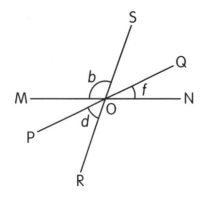

27 PQ, MN and XY are
straight lines.
∠a = ∠c = ∠e.
Find ∠b.

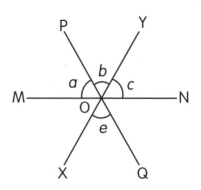

Practice Book 5B, p.103

Let's Wrap It Up!

You have learnt that:

- the sum of angles on a straight line is 180°
- the sum of angles at a point is 360°
- vertically opposite angles are equal.

Let's Revise!

ST, UV and KL are straight lines.
$\angle a = \angle c = \angle e$. What is the sum of $\angle b$, $\angle d$ and $\angle f$?

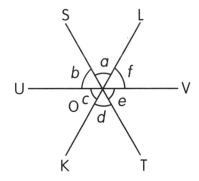

The sum of angles on a straight line is 180°. Therefore:
$\angle b + \angle a + \angle f = 180°$

Vertically opposite angles are equal. Therefore:
$\angle a = \angle d$
So $\angle b + \angle d + \angle f = 180°$.

Put On Your Thinking Caps!

The following diagrams are not drawn to scale.

28 In the diagram, AB is perpendicular to BD, CB is perpendicular to BE and ∠ABC = 2°.
Is DE a straight line?
Explain your answer.

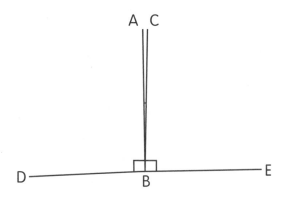

29 KL and PN are straight lines.

a Name another right angle in the diagram apart from ∠MON and ∠QOL.

b Name the angle equal to ∠KOM.
Explain why.

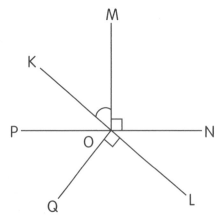

Practice Book 5B, p.105

Practice Book 5B, p.107

Properties of Triangles and 4-sided Shapes

Let's Learn!

Angles of a triangle

Activity

1   Draw any two triangles on a piece of paper and cut them out. Name the three angles of each triangle as shown.

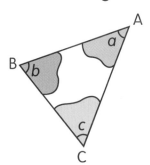

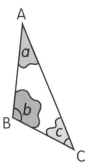

Cut out the three angles of your triangles and arrange them on a straight line as shown.

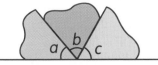

What can you say about the sum of the angles in a triangle?

$\angle a + \angle b + \angle c = 180°$

The sum of the angles on a straight line is 180°.

The sum of all the angles in a triangle is 180°.

Home Maths
Encourage your child to draw any three triangles and then measure the three angles in each triangle using a protractor. Then ask them to find the sum of the three angles in each triangle to confirm that they add up to 180°.

2 In triangle ABC, find ∠ACB.

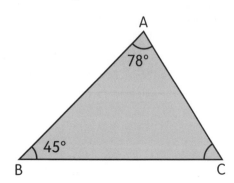

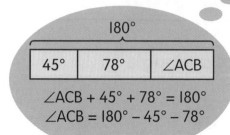

The sum of angles in a triangle = 180°.

180°

| 45° | 78° | ∠ACB |

∠ACB + 45° + 78° = 180°
∠ACB = 180° − 45° − 78°

∠ACB = 180° − 45° − 78°
     = 57°

3 Find the unknown marked angle in each triangle.

a

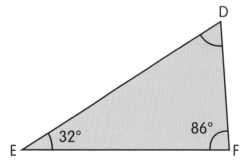

∠EDF = 180° − ☐° − ☐°

     = ☐°

The sum of angles in a triangle = 180°.
∠EDF + 32° + 86° = 180°

b

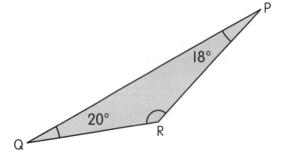

∠PRQ = ☐° − ☐° − ☐°

     = ☐°

Maths Journal

4   **a**   In triangle ABC, ∠BAC = 50°. Three possible examples of triangle ABC are shown. The triangles are not drawn to scale.

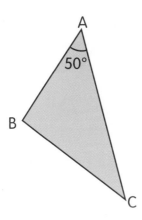
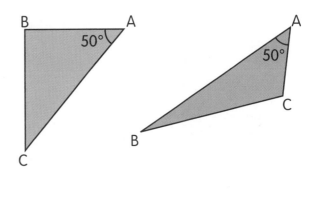

   i   What can you say about the sum of ∠ABC and ∠ACB?

   ii   State five possible sets of values for ∠ABC and ∠ACB.

   iii   Can ∠ABC equal 120°? Explain your answer.
   Can ∠ABC equal 130°? Explain your answer.

b   ∠x, ∠y and ∠z are the three angles of triangle XYZ.

   i   If ∠x is greater than 90°, can ∠y also be greater than 90°? Why?

   ii   If ∠x is greater than 90°, what can you say about ∠y and ∠z?

Let's Practise!

The following triangles are not drawn to scale. Find the unknown marked angles in each triangle.

5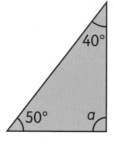

6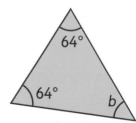

7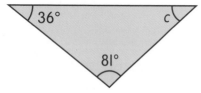

8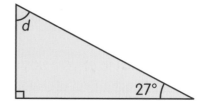

9

10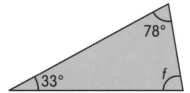

11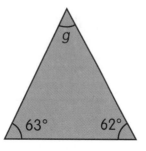

12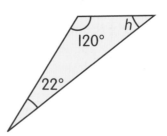

> Practice Book 5B, p.109

Let's Learn!

Right-angled, isosceles and equilateral triangles

Right-angled triangles

1 In triangle ABC, ∠ABC is a right angle.

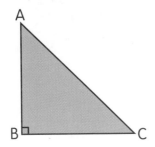

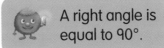

A right angle is equal to 90°.

Triangle ABC is called a **right-angled triangle**.

2 Here are three other examples of right-angled triangles.

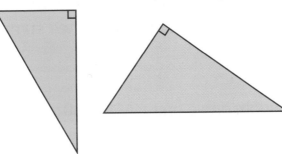

A right-angled triangle is a triangle in which one angle is a right angle.

Use a set-square to find out which of these are right-angled triangles.

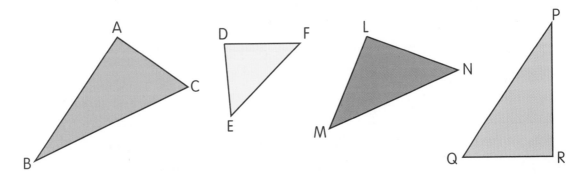

3 ABC is a right-angled triangle.

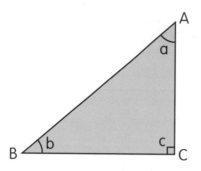

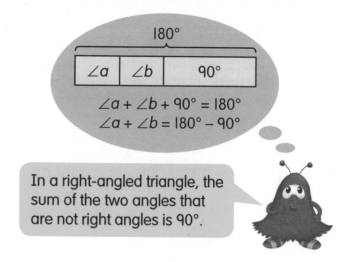

$$180°$$

∠a	∠b	90°

$$∠a + ∠b + 90° = 180°$$
$$∠a + ∠b = 180° - 90°$$

In a right-angled triangle, the sum of the two angles that are not right angles is 90°.

$∠c = 90°$
$∠a + ∠b + ∠c = 180°$
$∠a + ∠b + 90° = 180°$
$∠a + ∠b = 180° - 90°$
$\qquad\qquad = 90°$

4 Use a pencil and paper or the drawing tool in your computer to draw three right-angled triangles. Print them out. For each triangle, use a protractor to measure the angles that are not right angles. Find their sum. Do they add up to 90°?

5 In triangle ABC, ∠CAB is a right angle and ∠ACB = 60°. Find ∠ABC.

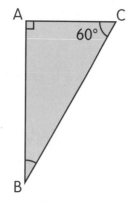

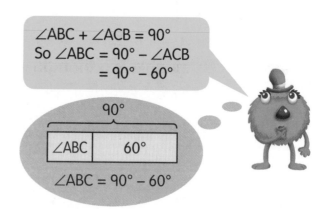

$$∠ABC + ∠ACB = 90°$$
$$So\ ∠ABC = 90° - ∠ACB$$
$$= 90° - 60°$$

$$90°$$

∠ABC	60°

$$∠ABC = 90° - 60°$$

$∠ABC = 90° - 60°$
$\qquad\quad = 30°$

Home Maths Ask your child to cut out a right-angled triangle from a rectangular piece of paper. Tear off the two angles which are not right angles and place them over the right angle. Do they fit exactly over the right angle?

6 The following triangles are not drawn to scale. Find the unknown angles in each of the right-angled triangles.

a

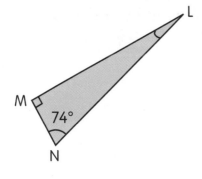

$\angle MLN = 90° - \boxed{}°$

$\quad\quad = \boxed{}°$

b

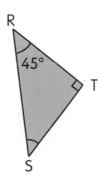

$\angle RST = 90° - \boxed{}°$

$\quad\quad = \boxed{}°$

c

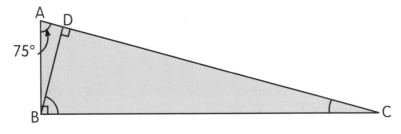

$\angle ACB = \boxed{}° - \boxed{}°$

$\quad\quad = \boxed{}°$

$\angle CBD = \boxed{}° - \boxed{}°$

$\quad\quad = \boxed{}°$

Let's Explore!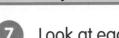

7 Look at each of these sets of three angles.

a 48°, 90°, 42°   b 29°, 72°, 90°
c 23°, 47°, 90°   d 90°, 31°, 59°

Which of these sets of angles can be angles of right-angled triangles?
What can you say about the angles of a right-angled triangle?

Practice Book 5B, p.III

119

Isosceles triangles

8 In triangle PQR, PQ = PR.

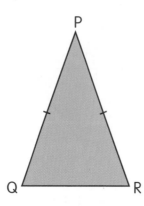

We mark the equal sides of the isosceles triangle like this:

Triangle PQR is called an **isosceles triangle**.

9 Here are three other examples of isosceles triangles.

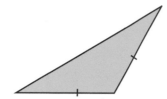 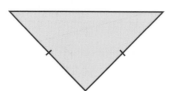 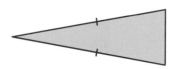

An isosceles triangle is a triangle in which two of the sides are equal.

Activity

10 Make a copy of the isosceles triangle ABC and cut it out.

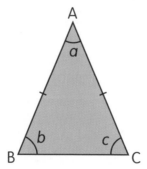

Activity

Fold your triangle along its line of symmetry.

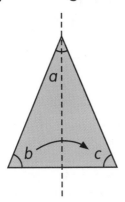

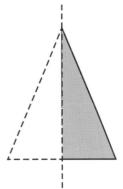

What can you say about the angles *b* and *c*?

In the isosceles triangle ABC, $\angle b = \angle c$.

In an isosceles triangle, the angles opposite the equal sides are equal.

Use a ruler or a protractor to find out which of these triangles are isosceles triangles.

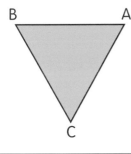

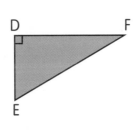

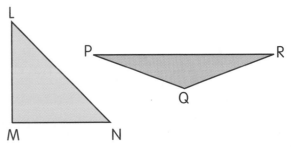

II The following triangles are not drawn to scale.

a In triangle ABC, AB = AC and $\angle ABC = 62°$. Find $\angle ACB$ and $\angle BAC$.

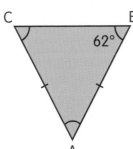

$\angle ACB = \angle ABC = 62°$ The angles opposite the equal sides are equal.

$\angle BAC = 180° - 62° - 62°$
$\qquad = 56°$

The sum of angles in a triangle is 180°.

b In triangle DEF, DE = DF and ∠EDF = 78°. Find ∠e and ∠f.

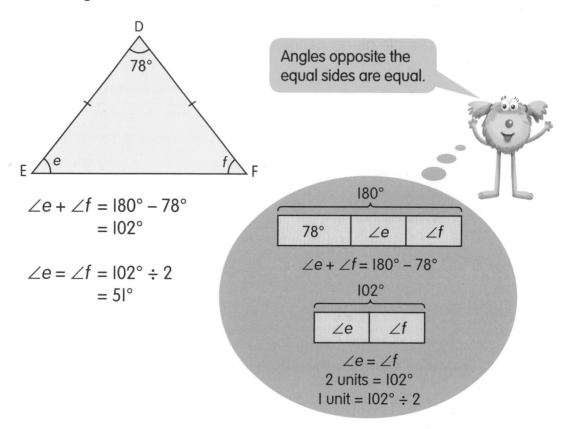

Angles opposite the equal sides are equal.

∠e + ∠f = 180° − 78°
    = 102°

∠e = ∠f = 102° ÷ 2
    = 51°

180°

| 78° | ∠e | ∠f |

∠e + ∠f = 180° − 78°
102°

| ∠e | ∠f |

∠e = ∠f
2 units = 102°
1 unit = 102° ÷ 2

12 The following triangles are not drawn to scale. Find the unknown marked angles.

a In triangle ABC, AB = AC and ∠ABC = 39°. Find ∠BAC.

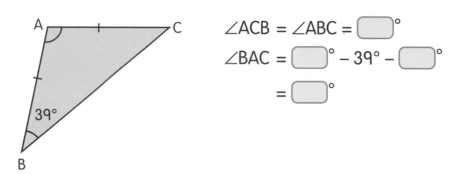

∠ACB = ∠ABC = ◯°

∠BAC = ◯° − 39° − ◯°

= ◯°

b In triangle DEF, DF = EF and ∠DFE = 74°. Find ∠DEF and ∠EDF.

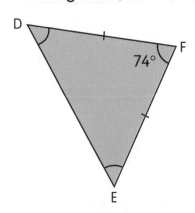

∠EDF + ∠DEF = ⬚° − ⬚°

= ⬚°

∠EDF = ∠DEF = ⬚° ÷ 2

= ⬚°

c In triangle ABC, AB = BC. Find ∠CBE.

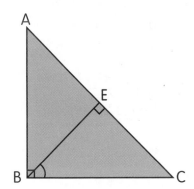

d In triangle ABC, ∠BAC = 90°, ∠ABD = 42° and AC = AD. Find ∠CAD.

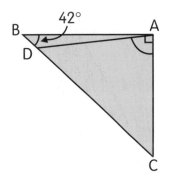

Practice Book 5B, p.113

Equilateral triangles

13 In triangle ABC, AB = BC = CA.

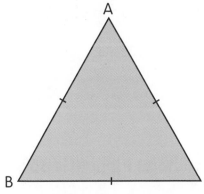

We mark the equal sides of the equilateral triangle like this:

Triangle ABC is called an **equilateral triangle**.

123

14 Here are three other examples of equilateral triangles.

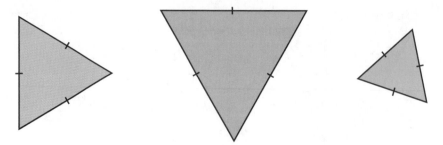

An equilateral triangle is a triangle in which the three sides are equal.

15 XYZ is an equilateral triangle.

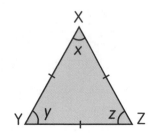

I can also think of an equilateral triangle as an isosceles triangle.

In an isosceles triangle, angles opposite the equal sides are equal.

In triangle XYZ, XY = XZ, YZ = YX, ZX = ZY.
So ∠y = ∠z, ∠z = ∠x, ∠x = ∠y. Therefore ∠x = ∠y = ∠z.

The angles of an equilateral triangle are equal.

∠x + ∠y + ∠z = 180°
∠x = ∠y = ∠z = 180° ÷ 3
            = 60°

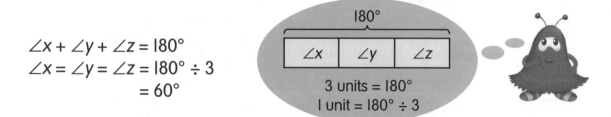

180°

| ∠x | ∠y | ∠z |

3 units = 180°
1 unit = 180° ÷ 3

Each angle in an equilateral triangle is 60°.

16 Which of the following triangles are equilateral triangles?

a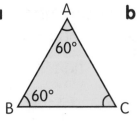

b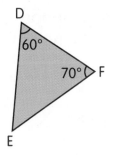

c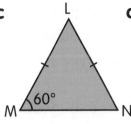

d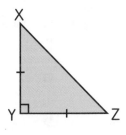

17 **a** ABC is an equilateral triangle. Find ∠BAD.

b ABD is an equilateral triangle. Find ∠ACB and ∠BDC.

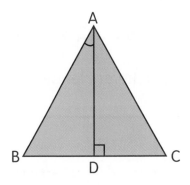

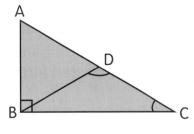

c ABC is an equilateral triangle. Find ∠ADE.

d PQR is an equilateral triangle. PS = PT. Find ∠PST.

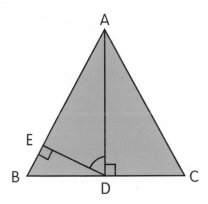

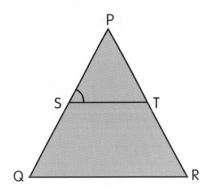

Let's Explore!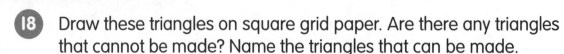

18 Draw these triangles on square grid paper. Are there any triangles that cannot be made? Name the triangles that can be made.

a A triangle with 2 equal sides and 1 angle greater than 90°.

b A triangle with 3 equal angles.

c A right-angled triangle with 3 equal sides.

d A right-angled triangle with 2 equal sides.

e A triangle with 2 equal sides and 3 angles less than 90°.

f A triangle with 3 sides of different lengths and 2 equal angles.

g A right-angled triangle with 3 sides of different lengths.

Maths Journal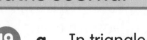

19 **a** In triangle PQR, PR = PQ. Write all you can about triangle PQR.

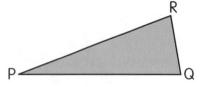

b In triangle XYZ, ∠XYZ = 43° and ∠XZY = 47°. Write all you can about triangle XYZ.

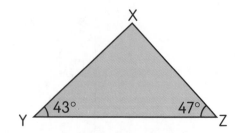

Let's Practise!

The following triangles are not drawn to scale.

20 ABC is an equilateral triangle. Find ∠ACB.

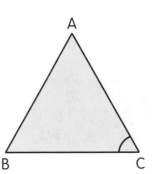

21 In triangle EFG, FE = FG. Find ∠GEF.

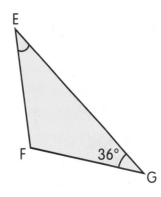

22 In triangle DEF, DE = DF and ∠EDF = 54°. Find ∠DFE.

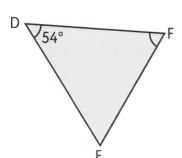

23 In triangle PQR, PR = QR and ∠QPR = 55°. Find ∠PRQ.

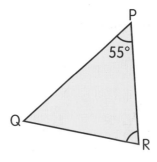

24 In triangle PQR, QP = QR. ∠PQR and ∠RSQ are right angles. Find ∠QPR and ∠RQS.

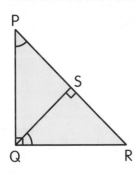

25 In triangle ABC, AC = BC. Find ∠ABE.

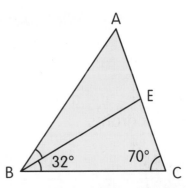

Practice Book 5B, p.115

127

Let's Learn!

> **Parallelograms, rhombuses and trapeziums**

Parallelograms

1 In the shape ABCD, AB is parallel to DC and BC is parallel to AD.

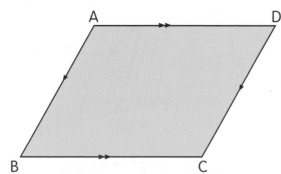

> I can write **AB is parallel to DC** as **AB // DC** and **BC is parallel to AD** as **BC // AD**.

The shape ABCD is called a **parallelogram**.

2 Here are three other examples of parallelograms.

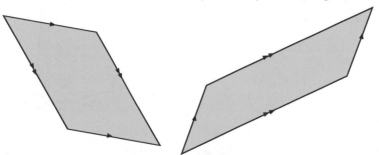

> **A parallelogram is a 4-sided shape in which the opposite sides are parallel.**

Use a ruler and a set-square to find out which of these shapes are **not** parallelograms.

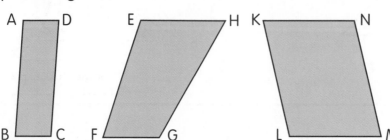
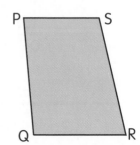

Activity

3 Your teacher will give you two copies of the parallelogram ABCD.

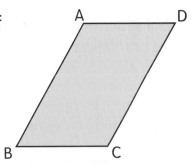

Cut one copy of the parallelogram into two pieces and slide one piece to match the sides AD and BC as shown.

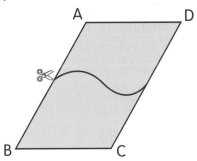

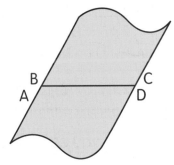

What can you say about the sides AD and BC?

In the same way, cut the other copy of the parallelogram into two pieces and slide one piece to match the sides AB and DC as shown.

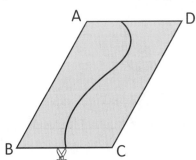

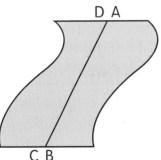

What can you say about the sides AB and DC?

In the parallelogram ABCD,

$$AD = BC \text{ and } AB = DC$$

Opposite sides of a parallelogram are equal.

Activity

4   Your teacher will give you two copies of the parallelogram PQRS.

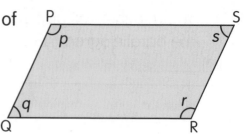

Cut one copy of the parallelogram into two pieces. Then make a half turn with one piece to match ∠p with ∠r and ∠q with ∠s as shown.

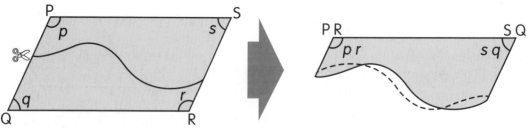

What can you say about ∠p and ∠r, ∠q and ∠s?

In parallelogram PQRS, ∠p = ∠r and ∠q = ∠s.

> **Opposite angles of a parallelogram are equal.**

Take the other copy of the parallelogram. Cut out the angles p, q, r and s from it as shown.

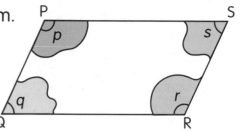

Put ∠p and ∠q together on a straight line as shown. In the same way, put ∠r and ∠s together.

What can you say about the sum of:

a   ∠p and ∠q?   **b**   ∠r and ∠s?

Activity

Now put ∠p and ∠s together on a straight line as shown. In the same way, put ∠r and ∠q together.

What can you say about the sum of:

c   ∠p and ∠s?   **d**   ∠r and ∠q?

$$∠p + ∠q = 180°   ∠p + ∠s = 180°$$
$$∠r + ∠s = 180°   ∠r + ∠q = 180°$$

Each pair of angles between two parallel sides of a parallelogram adds up to 180°.

5   Find the unknown marked angles in the parallelogram STUV.

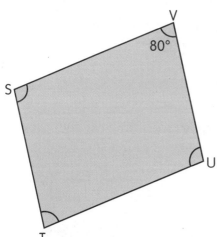

∠STU = ∠SVU = 80°

∠SVU and ∠STU are opposite angles.
∠SVU =∠STU

∠TUV = 180° − 80°
      = 100°

∠TUV and ∠SVU are a pair of angles between the parallel sides SV and TU.

∠VST = ∠TUV = 100°

∠VST and ∠TUV are opposite angles.
∠VST = ∠TUV

 When any one angle of a parallelogram is given, we are able to find all the other angles.

 Home Maths   Draw a parallelogram. Ask your child to measure the opposite sides to confirm that they are equal. Do the same for the opposite angles.

6 The following parallelograms are not drawn to scale. Find the unknown marked angles.

a Find ∠PQR.

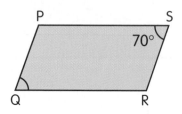

∠PQR = ∠⬚ = ⬚°

b Find ∠ABC.

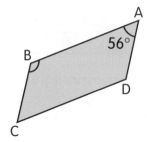

∠ABC = ⬚° − ⬚°
     = ⬚°

c Find ∠MQP and ∠NMQ.

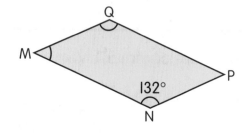

∠MQP = ∠⬚ = ⬚°
∠NMQ = ⬚° − ⬚°
     = ⬚°

d Find ∠WZY, ∠ZWX and ∠ZYX.

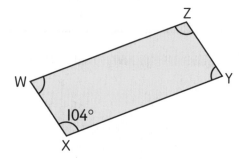

∠WZY = ∠⬚ = ⬚°
∠ZWX = ⬚° − ⬚°
     = ⬚°
∠ZYX = ∠⬚ = ⬚°

e PQRS is a parallelogram. Find ∠RQS.

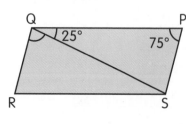

∠PQR = ⬚° − ⬚°
     = ⬚°
∠RQS = ∠⬚ − ∠PQS
     = ⬚° − ⬚°
     = ⬚°

∠PQR and ∠SPQ is a pair of angles between two parallel sides.

7 The parallelograms below are not drawn to scale.

a ABCD is a parallelogram.
Find ∠BDC.

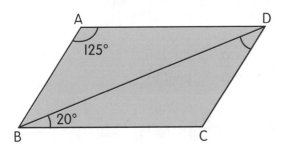

b PQRT is a parallelogram.
Find ∠SPT.

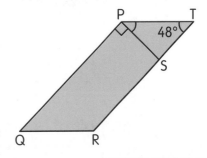

Practice Book 5B, p.119

Rhombuses

8 In the shape ABCD, AB is parallel to DC,
AD is parallel to BC and AB = BC = CD = DA.

The shape ABCD is called a **rhombus**.

Here are three more examples of rhombuses.

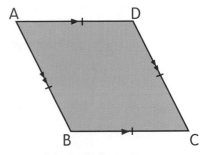

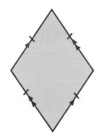

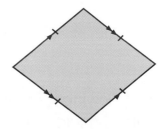

9 A rhombus is a 4-sided shape in which the opposite sides are parallel and all four sides are equal.

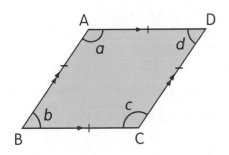

I can think of a rhombus as a parallelogram with four equal sides.

So in the rhombus ABCD, $\angle a = \angle c$ and $\angle b = \angle d$.

Opposite angles of a rhombus are equal.

$\angle a + \angle b = 180°$ $\angle a + \angle d = 180°$
$\angle c + \angle d = 180°$ $\angle b + \angle c = 180°$

Each pair of angles between the parallel sides of a rhombus adds up to 180°.

10 We can use the properties of a rhombus to find the unknown angles. In the rhombus ABCD:

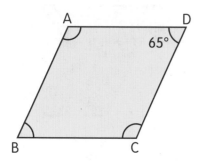

$\angle ABC = \angle ADC$
$\qquad = 65°$

> Opposite angles are equal.

$\angle BAD = 180° - 65°$
$\qquad = 115°$

> $\angle BAD$ and $\angle ADC$ are angles between two parallel sides.

$\angle DCB = \angle BAD$
$\qquad = 115°$

> $\angle DCB$ and $\angle BAD$ are opposite angles.

11 The following rhombuses are not drawn to scale. Find the unknown marked angles.

a Find $\angle FGH$.

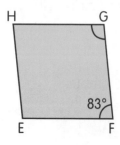

$\angle FGH = \boxed{}° - \boxed{}°$

$\qquad = \boxed{}°$

b Find $\angle KJL$.

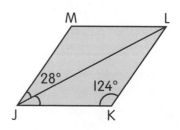

$\angle KJM = 180° - \boxed{}° = \boxed{}°$

$\angle KJL = \boxed{}° - 28° = \boxed{}°$

The following rhombuses are not drawn to scale.

12 ABCD is a rhombus. Find ∠DAB.

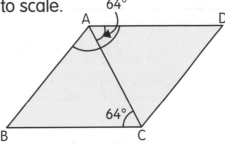

13 ABCD is a rhombus. Find ∠ABE.

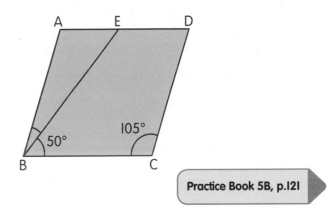

Practice Book 5B, p.121

Trapeziums

14 In the shape ABCD, AD // BC.

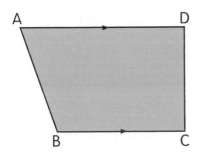

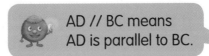

AD // BC means
AD is parallel to BC.

The shape ABCD is called a **trapezium**.

Here are three more examples of trapeziums.

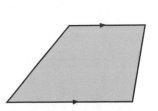

A trapezium is a 4-sided shape in which only one pair of opposite sides is parallel.

135

Activity

15 Your teacher will give you two copies of the trapezium ABCD.

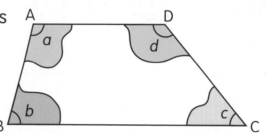

Cut out the angles *a*, *b*, *c* and *d*.

Arrange the cut-out pieces of ∠*a* and ∠*b* on a straight line as shown. In the same way, arrange the cut-out pieces of ∠*c* and ∠*d*.

What can you say about the sum of:

a ∠*a* and ∠*b*?   **b** ∠*c* and ∠*d*?

> ∠*a* +∠*b* = 180° and ∠*c* + ∠*d* = 180°

> **In a trapezium, each pair of angles between the parallel sides adds up to 180°.**

16 The following trapeziums are not drawn to scale. Find the unknown marked angles.

a

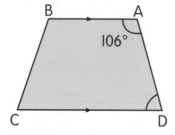

∠ADC = 180° − 106° = 74°

> ∠BAD and ∠ADC add up to 180°. They are a pair of angles between two parallel sides.

b

∠ZWX = 180° − 101°

= ◯ °

> ∠WXY and ∠ZWX add up to 180°.

The following trapeziums are not drawn to scale.

17 Find the unknown marked angles in trapezium KLMN.

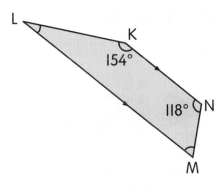

$\angle KLM = 180° - \boxed{}°$

$\qquad = \boxed{}°$

$\angle LMN = 180° - \boxed{}°$

$\qquad = \boxed{}°$

18 ABCD is a trapezium where AD // BC. Find $\angle$BAC.

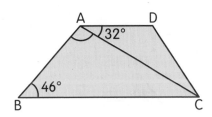

19 ABCD is a trapezium where AB // DC. Find $\angle$BCE.

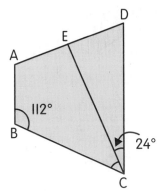

Maths Journal

20 Work in groups of four.
Compare the similarities and differences between the following:

	Similarities	Differences
1 a square and a rectangle		
2 a rectangle and a parallelogram		
3 a parallelogram and a rhombus		
4 a square and a rhombus		
5 a parallelogram and a trapezium		

Let's Practise!

The following shapes are not drawn to scale. Find the unknown marked angles.

21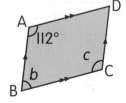

22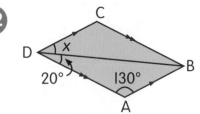

23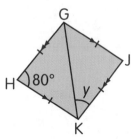

24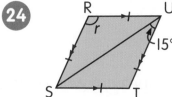

25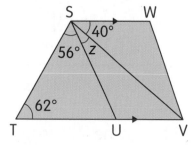

26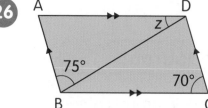

27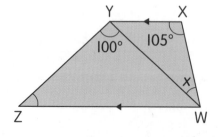

Practice Book 5B, p.123

Let's Wrap It Up!

You have learnt that:

- the sum of all the angles in a triangle is 180°
- in a right-angled triangle, the sum of the 2 angles which are not right angles is 90°
- an isosceles triangle has two equal sides and the angles opposite the equal sides are equal
- an equilateral triangle has three equal sides and each angle is 60°
- a parallelogram is a 4-sided shape in which:
    - **a** the opposite sides are parallel and equal
    - **b** the opposite angles are equal
    - **c** each pair of angles between two parallel sides adds up to 180°

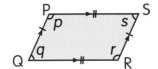

- a rhombus is a 4-sided shape in which:
    - **a** the opposite sides are parallel and all 4 sides are equal
    - **b** the opposite angles are equal
    - **c** each pair of angles between the parallel sides adds up to 180°

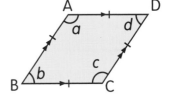

- a trapezium is a 4-sided shape in which:
    - **a** only one pair of opposite sides is parallel
    - **b** each pair of angles between the parallel sides adds up to 180°.

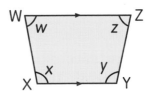

Let's Revise!

The shapes on the next page are not drawn to scale.
Find the unknown angles.

Let's Wrap It Up!

a Find ∠x.

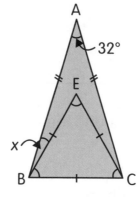

ABC is an isosceles triangle,
so ∠ABC = ∠ACB.
∠ABC = (180° − 32°) ÷ 2 = 74°
BCE is an equilateral triangle.
∠EBC = 60°
∠x = 74° − 60° = 14°

b ∠PSR = 65°. Find ∠d.

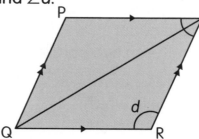

PQRS is a parallelogram.
∠QRS + ∠PSR = 180°
∠d + 65° = 180°
∠d = 180°− 65° = 115°

Put On Your Thinking Caps!

28 The shape below is not drawn to scale. It is made up of two right-angled triangles. Find the sum of the coloured angles.

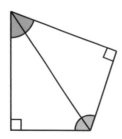

29 All the sides in the shape below are equal. Find the sum of all the unknown marked angles in the figure.

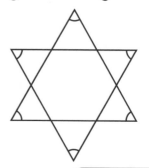

Practice Book 5B, p.126

Let's Learn!

Drawing triangles

1 Draw a triangle ABC in which BC = 5 cm, ∠ABC = 60° and ∠BCA = 50°.

Step 1 Using a ruler, draw BC = 5 cm.

B ——————————— C
5 cm

Step 2 Using a protractor, draw an angle of 60° at B.

Step 3 Using a protractor, draw an angle of 50° at C to locate the point A.

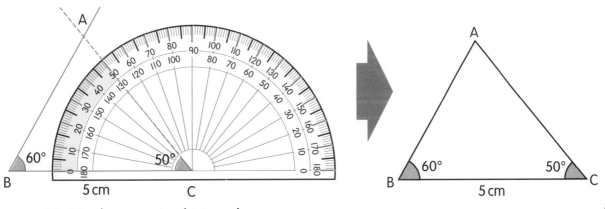

ABC is the required triangle.

2 Draw a triangle PQR in which QR = 6 cm, ∠PQR = 40° and ∠QRP = 75°.

Step I Using a ruler, draw
QR = ⬜ cm.

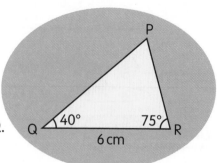

Step 2 Using a protractor,
draw an angle of ⬜° at Q.

Step 3 Using a protractor, draw an angle
of ⬜° at R to locate the point P .

3 Draw a triangle ABC in which AB = 4 cm, BC = 6 cm and ∠ABC = 45°.

Step I Using a ruler, draw BC = 6 cm.

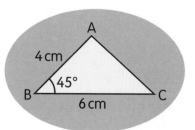

B ─────────────── C
6 cm

Step 2 Using a protractor, draw an angle of 45° at B.

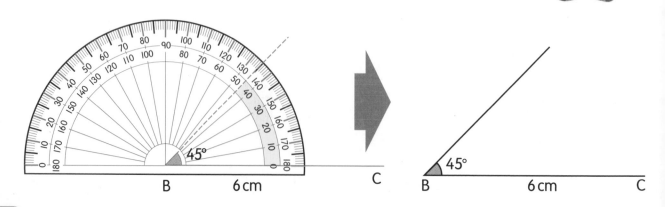

Step 3   Using a ruler, mark point A so that AB = 4 cm.

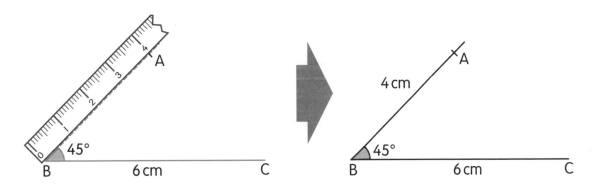

Step 4   Using a ruler, join AC.

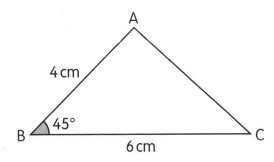

ABC is the required triangle.

4   Draw a triangle PQR in which QR = 7 cm, PR = 4 cm and ∠QRP = 50°.
Use the steps below to help you.

Step 1   Using a ruler, draw QR = ⬚ cm.

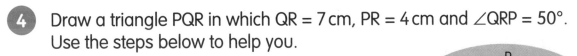

Step 2   Using a protractor, draw an angle
of ⬚° at R.

Step 3   Using a ruler, mark point P so that PR = ⬚ cm.

Step 4   Using a ruler, join PQ.

Activity

5 Work in pairs.

a Draw an isosceles triangle ABC in which AB = AC, BC = 6 cm and ∠BAC = 80°.
(Hint: Find ∠ABC and ∠BCA.)

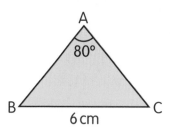

b Draw an equilateral triangle ABC with 6 cm sides.

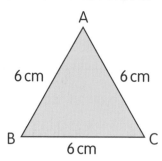

Let's Practise!

6 Draw each of the following triangles with the given measurements.

a
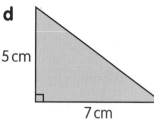

b
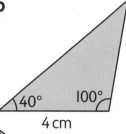

c
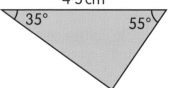

d

e
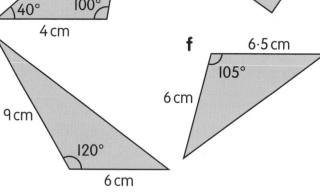

f

7 Draw a triangle ABC in which BC = 7 cm, ∠BCA = 50° and ∠CAB = 90°.

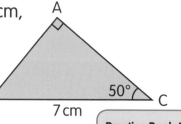

Practice Book 5B, p.135

Let's Learn!

Drawing 4-sided shapes

Drawing squares and rectangles

1 Draw a square ABCD with 3·5 cm sides.

    Step 1   Using a ruler, draw BC = 3·5 cm.

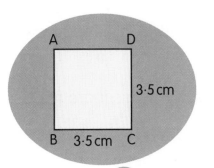

B ———————— C
             3·5 cm

    Step 2   Using a set-square, draw lines at B and C
                   perpendicular to BC.

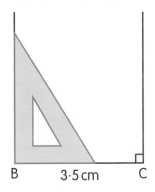  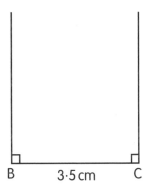

    Step 3   Using a ruler, mark points A and D so that BA = 3·5 cm
                   and CD = 3·5 cm.

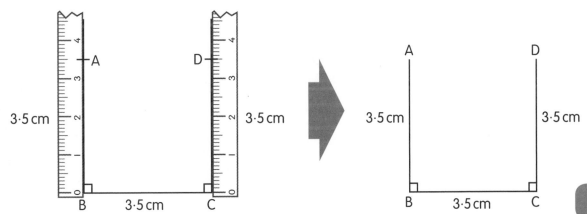

145

Step 4 Using a ruler, join AD.

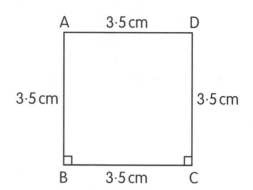

A   3·5 cm   D

3·5 cm   3·5 cm

B   3·5 cm   C

ABCD is the required square.

---

2   Draw a square ABCD with 4·5 cm sides.

Step 1 Using a ruler, draw AB = ⬭ cm.

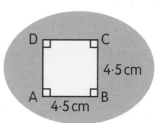

D   C

4·5 cm

A   B

4·5 cm

Step 2 Using a set-square and a ruler,
draw lines at A and B
perpendicular to ⬭.

Step 3 Using a ruler, mark points C and D so that
BC = ⬭ cm and AD = ⬭ cm.

Step 4 Using a ruler, join CD.

---

3   Draw a rectangle PQRS in which PQ = 4 cm and QR = 7 cm.

Step 1 Using a ruler, draw QR = ⬭ cm.

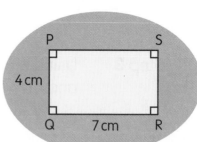

P   S

4 cm

Q   7 cm   R

Step 2 Using a set-square and a ruler,
draw lines at Q and R
perpendicular to ⬭.

Step 3 Using a ruler, mark points P and S so that
PQ = ⬭ cm and RS = ⬭ cm.

Step 4 Using a ruler, join ⬭.

Drawing rhombuses and parallelograms

4 Let's recall the properties of a rhombus and of a parallelogram.

A **rhombus** is a 4-sided shape.

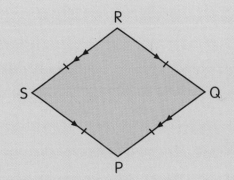

PQRS is a rhombus.
Its opposite sides are parallel.
So it has two pairs of parallel sides.
SP // RQ and RS // QP

It has 4 equal sides.
RS = SP = PQ = QR

Its opposite angles are equal.
∠QRS = ∠QPS and ∠PQR = ∠PSR

Each pair of angles between two parallel sides adds up to 180°.
∠QRS + ∠PSR = 180°   ∠PQR + ∠QRS = 180°
∠PQR + ∠QPS = 180°   ∠QPS + ∠PSR = 180°

A **parallelogram** is a 4-sided shape.

JKLM is a parallelogram.
Its opposite sides are parallel.
So it has two pairs of parallel sides.
KJ // LM and JM // KL

Its opposite sides are equal.
JK = ML and JM = KL

Its opposite angles are equal.
∠KJM = ∠KLM and ∠JKL = ∠JML

Each pair of angles between two parallel sides adds up to 180°.
∠KJM + ∠JKL = 180°   ∠KJM + ∠JML = 180°
∠JML + ∠KLM = 180°   ∠JKL + ∠KLM = 180°

5 Draw a rhombus ABCD with 4 cm sides and ∠ABC = 40°.

Step 1 Using a ruler, draw BC = 4 cm.

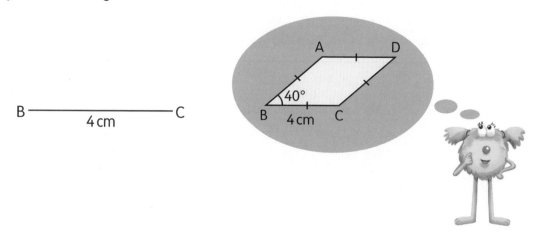

Step 2 Using a protractor, draw an angle of 40° at B.

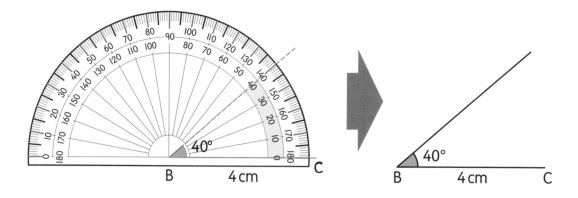

Step 3 Using a ruler, mark point A so that BA = 4 cm.

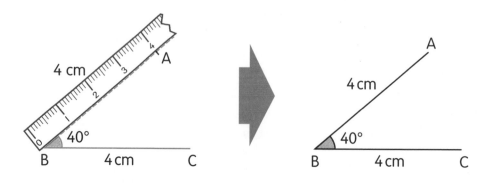

Step 4 Using a ruler and a set-square, draw a line through A parallel to BC.

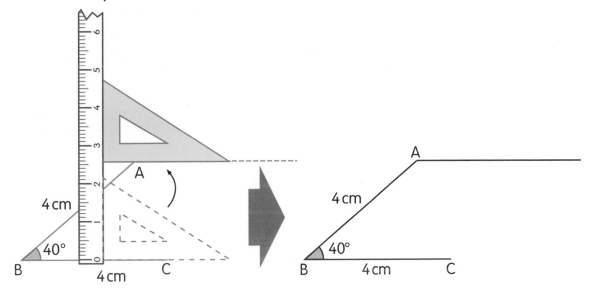

Step 5 Using a ruler, mark point D so that AD = 4 cm.

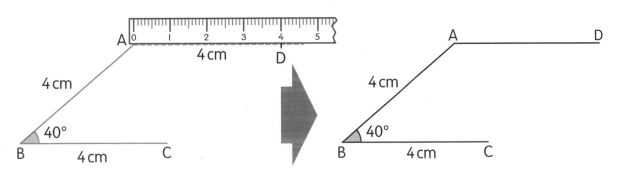

Step 6 Using a ruler, join CD.

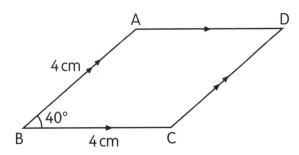

ABCD is the required rhombus.

6   Draw a parallelogram PQRS in which QR = 7 cm, PQ = 6 cm and
∠PQR = 70°. Use the steps below to help you.

Step 1   Using a ruler, draw QR = ☐ cm.

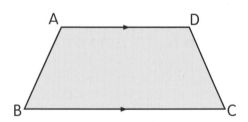

Step 2   Using a protractor, draw an
angle of ☐° at Q.

Step 3   Using a ruler, mark point P so that
PQ = ☐ cm.

Step 4   Using a ruler and a set-square, draw a line
through P parallel to ☐.

Step 5   Using a ruler, mark point S so that PS = ☐ cm.

Step 6   Using a ruler, join ☐ to get the required parallelogram PQRS.

Drawing trapeziums

7   Let's recall the properties of a trapezium.

A **trapezium** is a 4-sided shape.

ABCD is a trapezium.
One pair of opposite sides is parallel.
AD // BC

Each pair of angles between the parallel sides adds up to 180°.
∠ABC + ∠BAD = 180°
∠BCD + ∠ADC = 180°

8 Draw a trapezium ABCD in which AD // BC, AB = 4 cm, BC = 6 cm,
∠ABC = 35° and ∠BCD = 60°.

Step 1 Using a ruler, draw BC = 6 cm.

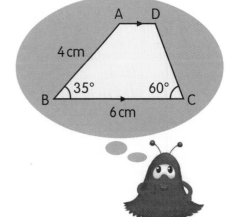

B ——————————— C
6 cm

Step 2 Using a protractor, draw an angle of 35° at B.

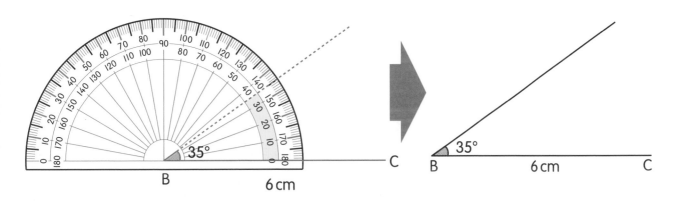

Step 3 Using a ruler, mark the point A so that BA = 4 cm.

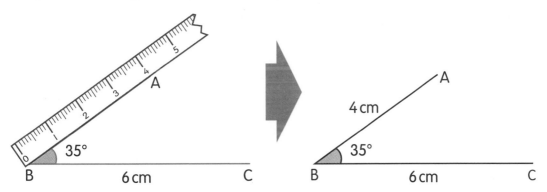

Step 4   Using a ruler and a set-square, draw a line through A parallel to BC.

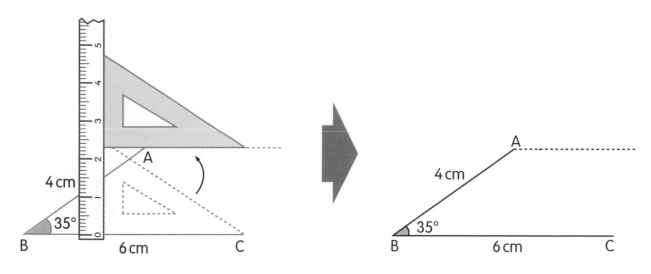

Step 5   Using a protractor, draw an angle of 60° at C. Mark the point D as shown.

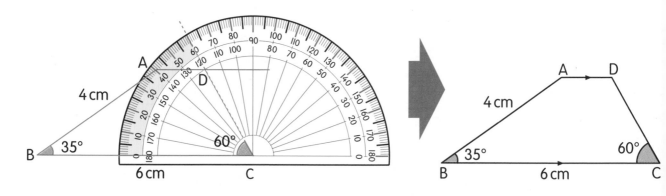

ABCD is the required trapezium.

9 Draw a trapezium EFGH in which EH // FG, FG = 6 cm, EF = 4 cm, ∠EFG = 95° and ∠FGH = 120°.

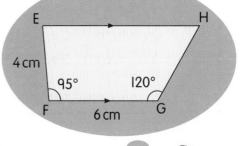

Step 1 Using a ruler, draw FG = ☐ cm.

Step 2 Using a protractor, draw an angle of ☐° at F.

Step 3 Using a ruler, mark point E so that FE = 4 cm.

Step 4 Using a ruler and a set-square, draw a line through E parallel to FG.

Step 5 Using a protractor, draw an angle of ☐° at G. Mark the point H to get the required trapezium EFGH.

Let's Practise!

10 Draw each of the following shapes with the given measurements.

a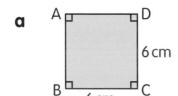

b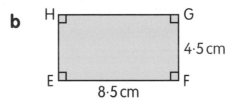

11 Draw a parallelogram JKLM and a rhombus PQRS with the given measurements.

a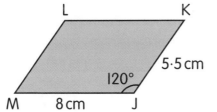

b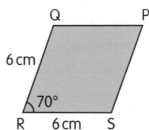

Let's Practise!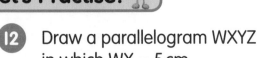

12 Draw a parallelogram WXYZ in which WX = 5 cm, WZ = 6 cm and ∠XWZ = 110°.

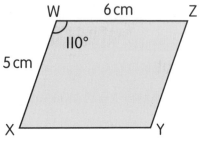

13 Draw a trapezium PQRS in which PS // QR, QR = 6·5 cm, RS = 3 cm, ∠PQR = 50° and ∠QRS = 70°.

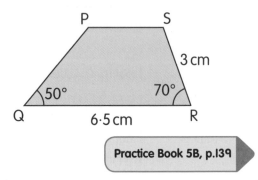

Practice Book 5B, p.139

Let's Wrap It Up!

You have learnt to use a ruler, protractor and set square:

- to draw a triangle given the required sides and angles
- to draw a square given one side
- to draw a rectangle given the length and width
- to draw a rhombus, a parallelogram and a trapezium given the required sides and angles.

Put On Your Thinking Caps!

14 Draw a triangle ABC in which AB = 8 cm, BC = 8 cm and ∠ABC = 60°. Measure the side AC. What can you conclude about the triangle ABC?

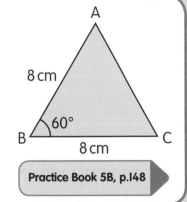

Practice Book 5B, p.148

Unit 14 Volume of Cubes and Cuboids

Let's Learn!

Building solids using unit cubes

1. The solid shown is a cube.
   A single cube is called a unit cube.

   A cube has square faces.

   Count the number of faces on a cube.

   It has ☐ faces.

   Face

   Edge

   Since each face is a square, all the edges are equal.

   Count the number of edges on a cube.

   It has ☐ edges.

2. This is another unit cube.

3. We can build solids using unit cubes.
   This solid is made up of 2 unit cubes.

   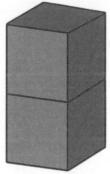

 Home Maths Encourage your child to find objects which are cubes and confirm the number of faces and edges with them.

4 Each of these solids is made up of ☐ unit cubes.

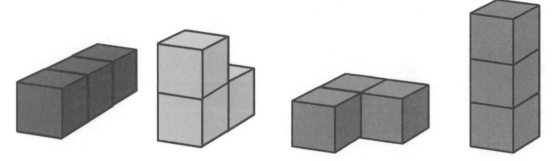

Activity

5 Use unit cubes to build each solid.

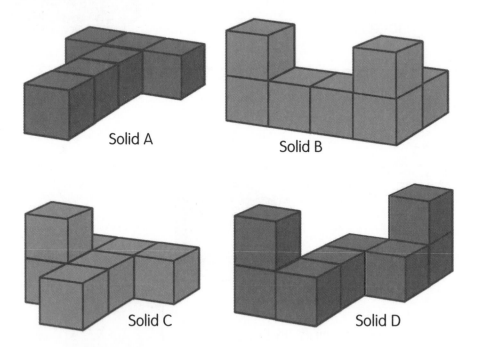

Solid A

Solid B

Solid C

Solid D

How many unit cubes did you use?

Solid A is made up of ☐ unit cubes.

Solid B is made up of ☐ unit cubes.

Solid C is made up of ☐ unit cubes.

Solid D is made up of ☐ unit cubes.

6 Use unit cubes to build this rectangular solid.

The rectangular solid is made up of ⬚ unit cubes.

Let's Explore!

7 Work in groups of four.
Your teacher will give each group 16 unit cubes.

To build a solid using two or more unit cubes, at least one face of
a unit cube must completely cover the face of another unit cube.
Here are examples of the same solid built using two unit cubes.

Example

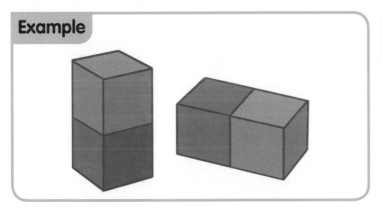

These are two views
of the same solid.

a Build as many different solids as you can using 3 unit cubes.
How many different solids can you build?

b Build as many different solids as you can using 4 unit cubes.
How many different solids can you build?

Let's Practise!

How many unit cubes are used to build each solid?

8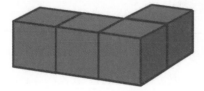

Number of unit cubes = ☐

9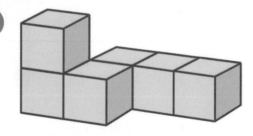

Number of unit cubes = ☐

10

Number of unit cubes = ☐

11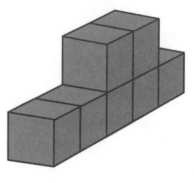

Number of unit cubes = ☐

Practice Book 5B, p.149

Let's Learn!

Drawing cubes and cuboids

1 This is a drawing of a unit cube on dotty paper.

2 When another unit cube is drawn as shown, we get a cuboid.

A **cuboid** is a rectangular solid.

3 Copy the cuboids in **2** on a piece of dotty paper. In each case, draw another unit cube to make a larger cuboid.

4 These are drawings of other cubes and cuboids.

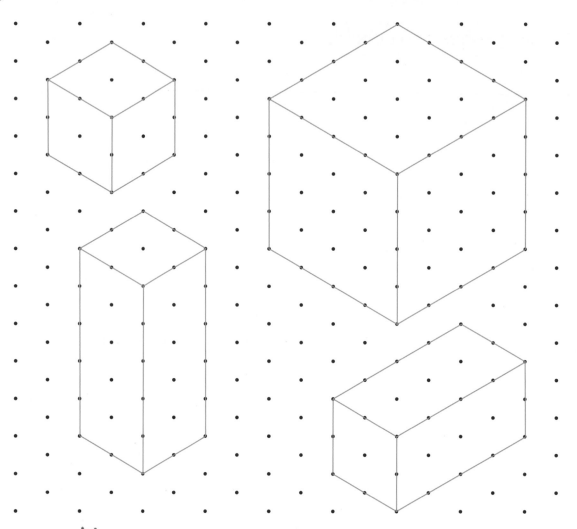

Activity

5 Draw these solids on a piece of dotty paper.

a b c

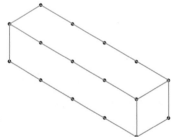
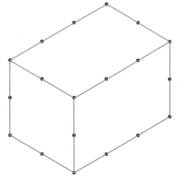

Activity

6 Copy each partly-drawn cube or cuboid on a piece of dotty paper.
Then complete the drawing.

a

b

c

Let's Practise!

Use dotty paper for these questions.

7 Draw the solids below.

a

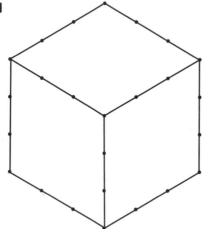

b

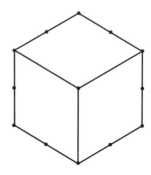

c

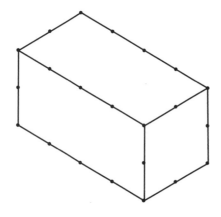

d

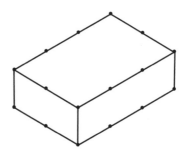

8 Draw a cube with edges 3 times as long as this unit cube.

Let's Practise!

9 Complete the drawing of each cube or cuboid.

a

b

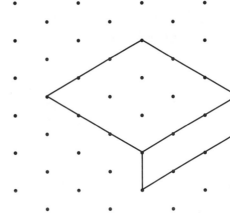

c

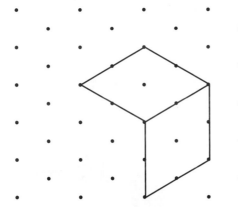

d

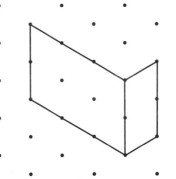

Practice Book 5B, p.151

Let's Learn!

> ### Understanding and measuring volume

1

> The watermelon takes up more space than the orange in the fridge.

> This is because the watermelon has a greater volume than the orange.

 The **volume** of a solid is the amount of space it occupies.

2 Which object has a greater volume?

tennis ball

OR

rugby ball

a The ⬚ has a greater volume.

 Home Maths Encourage your child to compare the mass and volume of various objects. Note that a lighter object can have a bigger volume.

b

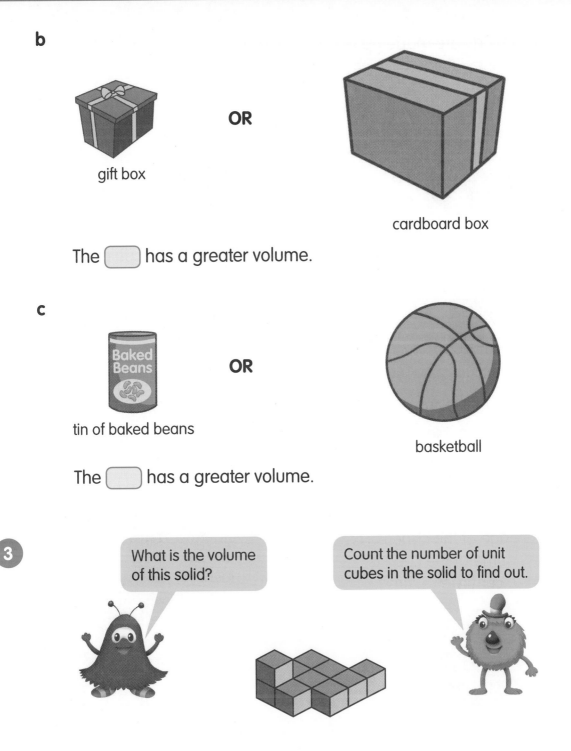

OR

gift box

cardboard box

The ⬭ has a greater volume.

c

tin of baked beans

OR

basketball

The ⬭ has a greater volume.

3

What is the volume of this solid?

Count the number of unit cubes in the solid to find out.

The solid is built using 10 unit cubes.
The volume of a unit cube is 1 **cubic unit**.
The volume of the solid is 10 cubic units.

4 These solids are made up of unit cubes.
What is the volume of each solid?

a

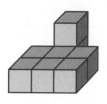

Volume = ☐ cubic units

b

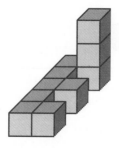

Volume = ☐ cubic units

c

Volume of cube
= ☐ cubic units

d

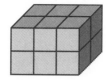

Volume of cuboid
= ☐ cubic units

5 This is a 1 cm cube.
Each edge of the cube is 1 cm long.
The volume of the cube is
1 **cubic centimetre (cm³)**.

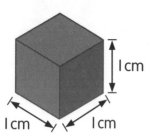

1 cm

1 cm   1 cm

The cubic centimetre
(cm³) is a unit of
measurement for volume.

6 These solids are made up of I cm cubes.
Find the volume of each solid.

a

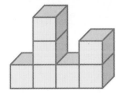

Volume = ⬚ cm³

b

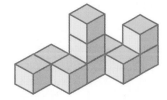

Volume = ⬚ cm³

7 **a** This cuboid is made up of twelve I cm cubes.

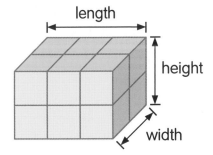

Length of cuboid = (I + I + I) cm = 3 cm
Width of cuboid = (I + I) cm = 2 cm
Height of cuboid = (I + I) cm = 2 cm
Volume of cuboid = 12 cm³

b This cuboid is made up of I cm cubes.

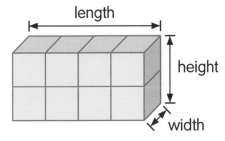

Length of cuboid = ⬚ cm
Width of cuboid = ⬚ cm
Height of cuboid = ⬚ cm
Volume of cuboid = ⬚ cm³

8 This is a 1m cube.
Each edge of the cube is 1m long.
Its volume is 1 **cubic metre (m³)**.

The cubic metre (m³) is also a unit of measurement for volume.

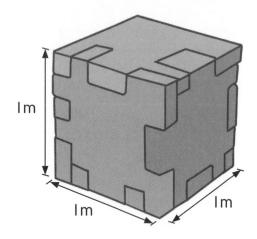

1m

1m   1m

9 These solids are made up of 1m cubes.
Find the volume of each solid.

a

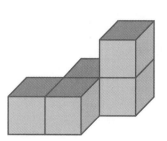

Volume = ⬭ m³

b

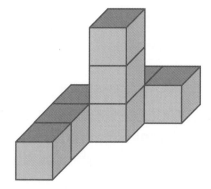

Volume = ⬭ m³

10 This cuboid is made up of 1m cubes.
What is its volume?

There are ⬭ 1m cubes in this cuboid.

Its volume is ⬭ m³.

Its length is ⬭ m.

Its width is ⬭ m.

Its height is ⬭ m.

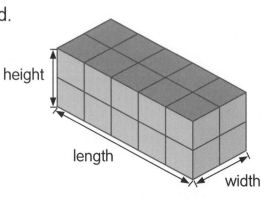

height

length

width

Activity

11 Work in pairs.
Your teacher will give each pair twelve 1 cm cubes.

a Make this cuboid using all the
1 cm cubes.
What is the volume of the
cuboid?

Volume = ⬚ cm³

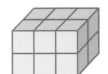

b Rearrange the 1 cm cubes to
build Solid A.
What is the volume of Solid A?

Volume = ⬚ cm³

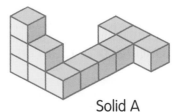

Solid A

c Rearrange the 1 cm cubes to
build Solid B.
What is the volume of Solid B?

Volume = ⬚ cm³

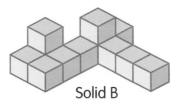

Solid B

d Build two more different solids using the 1 cm cubes.
What is the volume of each solid?
What do you notice?

Different solids can have the ⬚ volume.

Let's Explore!

12   Work in groups of four.
Your teacher will give each group 24 of the 1 cm cubes.
Build all the possible cubes and cuboids using 8, 11 and 12 of the 1 cm cubes.

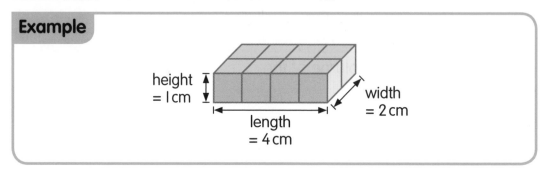

Example

height = 1 cm
width = 2 cm
length = 4 cm

Write down the length, width and height of the cubes and cuboids built. Then find the volume. On a sheet of paper, copy the table below and record your answers in it.

Number of 1 cm Cubes	Length	Width	Height	Volume
8	4	2	1	8
	☐	☐	☐	☐
	☐	☐	☐	☐
11	☐	☐	☐	☐
12	☐	☐	☐	☐
	☐	☐	☐	☐
	☐	☐	☐	☐
	☐	☐	☐	☐

What do you notice when you multiply the length by the width and by the height of each cube or cuboid?

Let's Practise!

13 These solids are made up of I cm cubes. Find their volumes.

a

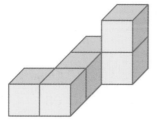

Volume = ⬭ cm³

b

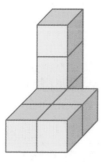

Volume = ⬭ cm³

c

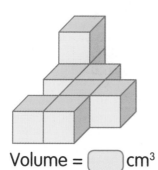

Volume = ⬭ cm³

d

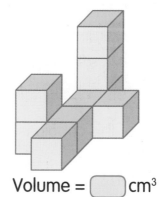

Volume = ⬭ cm³

14 These cuboids are built using I m cubes. What are the missing values?

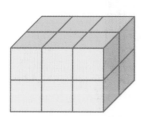

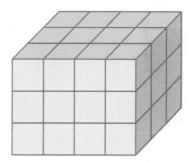

Volume = ⬭ m³
Length = ⬭ m
Width = ⬭ m
Height = ⬭ m

Volume = ⬭ m³
Length = ⬭ m
Width = ⬭ m
Height = ⬭ m

Practice Book 5B, p.155

Let's Learn!

Volume of a cuboid and of liquid

Volume of a cuboid

1 A cuboid is a rectangular solid.
All the faces of a cuboid are either rectangles or squares.

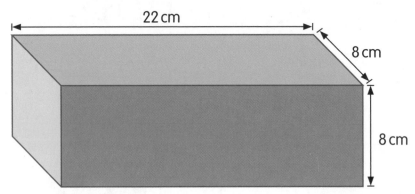

22 cm

8 cm

8 cm

The length of this cuboid is 22 cm.
Its width is 8 cm.
Its height is 8 cm.

2 What is the length, width and height of each cuboid?

a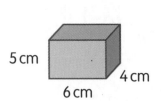

5 cm

6 cm

4 cm

b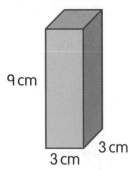

9 cm

3 cm

3 cm

Length = ⬚ cm

Width = ⬚ cm

Height = ⬚ cm

Length = ⬚ cm

Width = ⬚ cm

Height = ⬚ cm

Home
Maths

Encourage your child to name five objects
around the house which are cuboids.

c

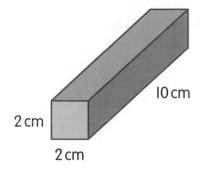

10 cm

2 cm

2 cm

Length = ⬡ cm

Width = ⬡ cm

Height = ⬡ cm

d

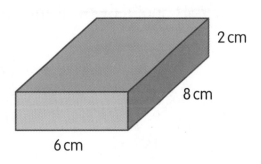

2 cm

8 cm

6 cm

Length = ⬡ cm

Width = ⬡ cm

Height = ⬡ cm

3 This cuboid is made up of 1 cm cubes.

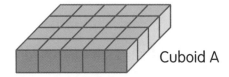

Cuboid A

There are 20 of the 1 cm cubes in Cuboid A.
The volume of Cuboid A is 20 cm³.

Add another layer of 1 cm cubes to build Cuboid B.

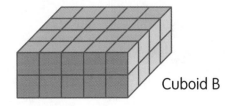

Cuboid B

There are 2 layers of 1 cm cubes.
Each layer is made up of 20 of the 1 cm cubes.
20 + 20 = 40
There are 40 of the 1 cm cubes in Cuboid B.

The volume of Cuboid B is ⬡ cm³.

4 Here is another way of finding the volume of Cuboid B.

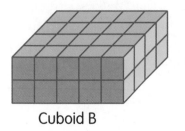  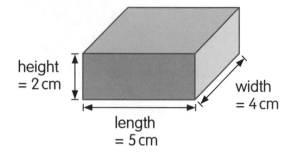

Cuboid B

height = 2 cm

length = 5 cm

width = 4 cm

The length of Cuboid B is 5 cm.
Its width is 4 cm.
Its height is 2 cm.

In 1 layer, there are $5 \times 4 = 20$ of the 1 cm cubes.
In 2 layers, there are $20 \times 2 = 5 \times 4 \times 2 = 40$ of the 1 cm cubes.
Volume of Cuboid B = $5 \times 4 \times 2 = 40 \, cm^3$

Volume of cuboid = Length × Width × Height

5 Find the volume of this cuboid.

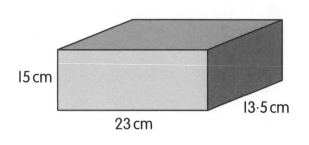

15 cm

23 cm

13·5 cm

Press	Display
C	0
2 3	23
× 1 3 · 5	13.5
× 1 5	15
=	4657.5

Length = 23 cm
Width = 13·5 cm
Height = 15 cm

Volume of cuboid = Length × Width × Height
= $23 \times 13 \cdot 5 \times 15$
= $4657 \cdot 5 \, cm^3$

6 A cube has edges 6 cm long. Find its volume.

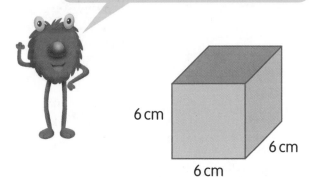

A cube is a cuboid in which the length, width and height are equal.

6 cm

6 cm

6 cm

Length = 6 cm
Width = 6 cm
Height = 6 cm

Volume of cube
= Length × Width × Height
= 6 × 6 × 6
= 216 cm³

7 Find the volume of a cube with edges of 14 cm.

Volume of cube = ☐ × ☐ × ☐
= ☐ cm³

Volume of a cube is equal to edge × edge × edge.

8 Find the volume of these cubes.

a Edge of cube = 22 cm

b Edge of cube = 13 m

9 Find the volume of these cuboids.

a Length = 26 cm
Width = 12 cm
Height = 8·25 cm

b Length = 15 m
Width = 14·02 m
Height = 9 m

Practice Book 5B, p.159

Volume of liquid

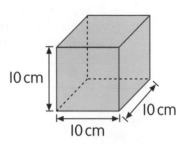

I litre of liquid completely fills a cuboid container 10 cm long, 10 cm wide and 10 cm high.

Recall that:
$1\ell = 1000\,\text{ml}$.

Volume of liquid in the container = $10 \times 10 \times 10 = 1000\,\text{cm}^3$
So $1000\,\text{ml} = 1000\,\text{cm}^3$
$1\,\text{ml} = 1\,\text{cm}^3$

11 Write in cubic centimetres.

  a $850\,\text{ml} = \boxed{}$ **b** $2\ell = \boxed{}$

  c $4\ell\ 55\,\text{ml} = \boxed{}$ **d** $12\ell\ 5\,\text{ml} = \boxed{}$

12 Write in litres and millilitres.

  a $530\,\text{cm}^3 = \boxed{}$ **b** $1025\,\text{cm}^3 = \boxed{}$

  c $7005\,\text{cm}^3 = \boxed{}$ **d** $15\,060\,\text{cm}^3 = \boxed{}$

Home Maths   At the supermarket, encourage your child to find five different products and the volume of their contents in litres or millilitres.

Activity

13 Work in groups of 4.
Your teacher will give each group 4 different small containers.
Your teacher will prepare a bucket of water and provide each group with a square container 10 cm long, 10 cm wide and 10 cm high.

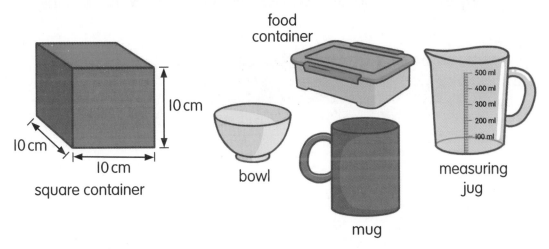

food
container

10 cm

10 cm

10 cm

square container

bowl

mug

measuring
jug

Follow these steps to find the capacity of each of the four containers the group has.

1 Fill the container completely with water.

2 Pour the water from the container into the given square container.

3 Using a ruler, measure the depth of the water in the square container correct to the nearest centimetre.

4 Use your knowledge on finding the volume of a cuboid to find the capacity of the container in millilitres.

Then record your answers in a table as shown.

Example

Container	Depth of Water in Square Container	Capacity of Container (ml)
Mug	6 cm	$10 \times 10 \times 6 = 600$ $= 600\,cm^3$ $= 600\,ml$

Let's Explore!

14 Work in pairs.
A cuboid has its length, width and height measured in whole centimetres.
Its volume is 120 cm³ and its length is 5 cm.
Copy the table and fill in possible values of the width and the height of the cuboid.

Length (cm)	Width (cm)	Height (cm)	Volume (cm³)
5			120
5			120
5			120
5			120

Practice Book 5B, p.163

Word problems

15 A cuboid container measures 15 cm by 10 cm by 8 cm.
It is completely filled with water.
How many litres and millilitres of water are there in the container?

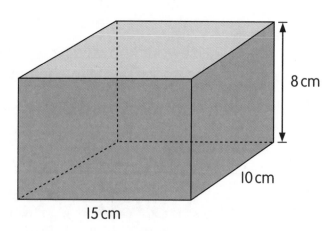

8 cm

10 cm

15 cm

Volume of water in the container = 15 × 10 × 8 = 1200 cm³
$$= 1200 \text{ ml} = 1 \ell \ 200 \text{ ml}$$

There is 1 ℓ 200 ml of water in the container.

16 A cuboid box measures 26 cm by 15 cm by 12·5 cm.
Find the capacity of the box in litres and millilitres.

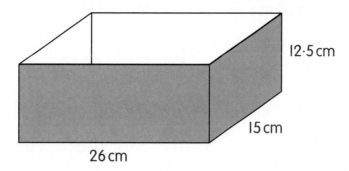

12·5 cm

15 cm

26 cm

Capacity of box = ⬚ × ⬚ × ⬚

= ⬚ cm³

= ⬚ ml

= ⬚ ℓ ⬚ ml

The capacity of the box is ⬚.

17 The edge of a cubical tin is 15 cm long. It contains 1·25 litres of water.
How much more water is needed to fill the tin completely? Give your
answer in litres. (1 ℓ = 1000 cm³)

Capacity of tin = 15 × 15 × 15

= 3375 cm³

= 3375 ml

= 3·375 ℓ

Volume of water in tin = 1·25 ℓ

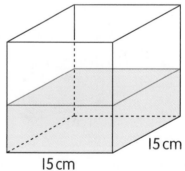

15 cm

15 cm

Amount of water needed to fill the tin = 3·375 − 1·25
= 2·125 ℓ

2·125 ℓ of water is needed to fill the tin completely.

18 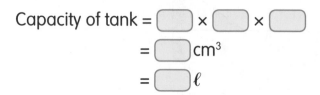 There is 1·75 ℓ of water in a cuboid container. The base of the container is a square with 12 cm sides and its height is 16·5 cm. How much more water is needed to fill the container to the brim? (1 ℓ = 1000 cm³)

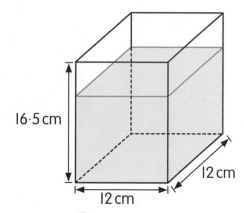

Capacity of tank = ⬭ × ⬭ × ⬭

= ⬭ cm³

= ⬭ ℓ

16·5 cm

12 cm

12 cm

Volume of water in container = ⬭ ℓ

Amount of water needed to fill the container = ⬭ ◯ ⬭ = ⬭ ℓ

⬭ ℓ of water is needed to fill the container to its brim.

19 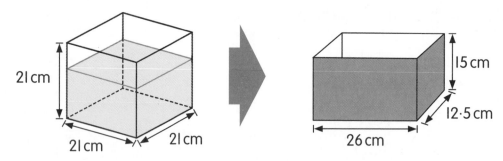 A cubical tank with 21 cm edges is $\frac{2}{3}$ filled with water. The water is then poured into a cuboid tank 26 cm by 12·5 cm by 15 cm until it is full. How much water is left in the cubical tank? Give your answer in millilitres. (1 cm³ = 1 ml)

21 cm

21 cm   21 cm

15 cm

12·5 cm

26 cm

Volume of water in the cubical tank = $\frac{2}{3}$ × 21 × 21 × 21

= 6174 cm³ = 6174 ml

Capacity of cuboid tank = 26 × 12·5 × 15

= 4875 cm³ = 4875 ml

Amount of water left in the cubical tank = 6174 − 4875 = 1299 ml

The cubical tank has 1299 ml of water left.

20 A cuboid tank 45 cm long, 28 cm wide and 30 cm high is filled with water up to $\frac{1}{4}$ of its height. Water from a tap flows into the tank at 2·5 litres a minute. How much water is in the tank after 5 minutes? Give your answer in litres. ($1\,\ell = 1000\,cm^3$)

Volume of water in tank

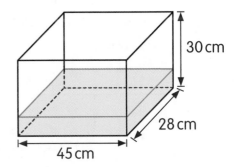

30 cm

28 cm

45 cm

= ⬭ × ⬭ × ⬭ × ⬭

= ⬭ cm³ = ⬭ ℓ

Volume of water from the tap = ⬭ × ⬭ = ⬭ ℓ

Volume of water in tank after 5 minutes = ⬭ ◯ ⬭ = ⬭ ℓ

⬭ ℓ of water is in the tank after 5 minutes.

Let's Explore!

21 Three pieces of cardboard, each 16 cm by 4 cm, are folded along the dotted lines and placed on a table to make open rectangular boxes. Each box is fixed to the table with sticky tape and filled completely with sand.

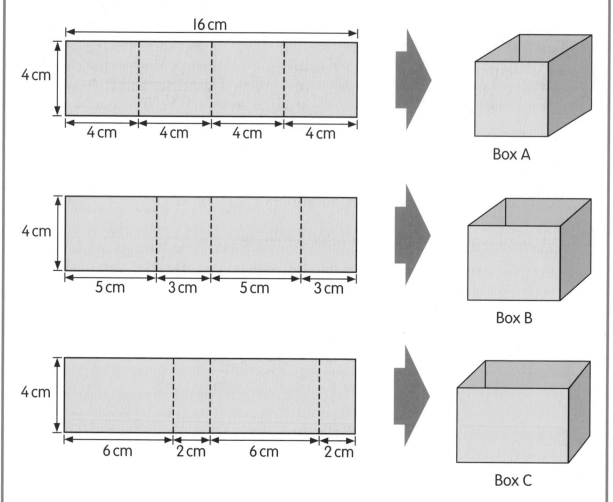

Box A

Box B

Box C

Find the volume of sand in each box.

a Are the volumes the same or different?

b If they are different which box has the largest volume of sand? What can you say about this box?

Let's Practise!

Solve these word problems. Show your workings clearly.

22 A cuboid is 29 cm long, 15 cm wide and 3·7 cm high. Find its volume.

23 A cuboid is 42 cm long, 32·4 cm wide and 26 cm high. Find its volume.

24 A cuboid tub measures 15 m by 11 m by 4·75 m. Find its capacity in cubic metres.

25 Find the volume of a cube with 21 m edges. Give your answer in cubic metres.

26 A cuboid tank 28 cm by 18 cm by 12 cm is filled to the brim with water. Then 0·78 ℓ of water from the tank is used up. How much water is left in the tank? Give your answer in millilitres. (1 ℓ = 1000 cm³)

27 A cuboid fish tank measures 55 cm by 24 cm by 22 cm. It contains 6·75 ℓ of water. How much more water is needed to fill the tank completely? Give your answer in litres. (1 ℓ = 1000 cm³)

28 A cuboid tank with a base that is a square with sides of 60 cm and a height of 45 cm. It is $\frac{1}{3}$ filled with water. Water from a tap flows into the tank at 6 litres per minute. How long will it take to fill the tank completely? (1 ℓ = 1000 cm³)

29 A cuboid tank 27 cm by 20 cm by 37·5 cm is half-filled with water. The water is poured into a cubical tank with 16 cm edges until it is $\frac{3}{4}$ full. How much water is left in the cuboid tank? Give your answer in litres to 1 decimal place. (1 ℓ = 1000 cm³)

> Practice Book 5B, p.165

Let's Wrap It Up!

You have learnt:

- to build solids using unit cubes
- to draw cubes and cuboids on dotty paper
- to state what the volume of a solid is
- to recognise that the volume of a solid, a cube or a cuboid is measured in cubic units, cm^3 or m^3
- **the volume of a cuboid = Length × Width × Height**
- to find the volume of liquid in a cuboid tank
- **1 litre = 1000 cm^3 and 1 ml = 1 cm^3**.

Let's Revise!

Jenny poured water into a cuboid container until it was $\frac{2}{3}$ filled. Then she poured some of the water out until it was $\frac{2}{5}$ filled. How much water did she pour out of the container? Give your answer in millilitres.

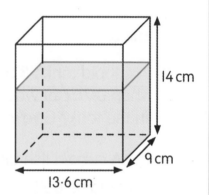

14 cm

9 cm

13·6 cm

Original volume of water = $13 \cdot 6 \times 9 \times 14 \times \frac{2}{3}$
$= 1142 \cdot 4 \, cm^3 = 1142.4 \, ml$

Final volume of water = $13 \cdot 6 \times 9 \times 14 \times \frac{2}{5}$
$= 685 \cdot 44 \, cm^3 = 685 \cdot 44 \, ml$

Volume of water poured out = $1142 \cdot 4 - 685 \cdot 44$
$= 456 \cdot 96 \, ml$

Jenny poured out 456·96 ml of water.

Put On Your Thinking Caps!

30 Work in pairs.

Your teacher will give each pair 15 unit cubes.

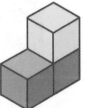

Staircase 1 Staircase 2 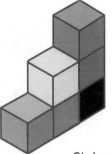 Staircase 3

a Look at the pattern of staircases made using unit cubes.
Build Staircases 4 and 5 using the unit cubes given.
Then record your answers in a table like this:

Staircase	Number of Unit Cubes
1	1
2	1 + 2 = 3
3	1 + 2 + 3 = 6
4	
5	

b Without building Staircase 6, find the number of unit cubes in it.

c Find the number of unit cubes in Staircase 8.

d If each unit cube has a of 1 cm edge, what are the volumes of Staircases 9 and 10?

Put On Your Thinking Caps!

31 These cuboids are built using 4 and 6 of the 1 cm cubes.

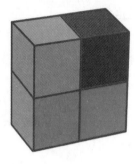 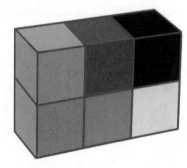

a How many different cuboids can you build using 5, 6, 7, 8 and 9 of the 1 cm cubes?

b List the length, width and height of each cuboid you built.

Practice Book 5B, p.171   Practice Book 5B, p.172